The Secret of the Bethlehem Shepherds

Also by Dwight Longenecker:

Immortal Combat

An Answer, Not an Argument

Our Lady? A Catholic/Evangelical Debate

St. Benedict and St. Thérèse: The Little Rule and The Little Way

Listen My Son: St. Benedict for Fathers

The Gargoyle Code

Beheading Hydra

Slubgrip Instructs

Catholicism Pure and Simple

More Christianity

The Mystery of the Magi

Praying the Rosary for Inner Healing

Praying the Rosary for Spiritual Warfare

A Sudden Certainty

The Quest for the Creed

The Romance of Religion

Letters on Liturgy

FR. DWIGHT LONGENECKER

The Secret of the Bethlehem Shepherds

SOPHIA INSTITUTE PRESS

Manchester, New Hampshire

Sophia Institute Press
Box 5284, Manchester, NH 03108
1-800-888-9344

www.SophiaInstitute.com

Sophia Institute Press® is a registered trademark of Sophia Institute.

paperback ISBN 978-1-64413-804-5

ebook ISBN 978-1-64413-805-2

Library of Congress Control Number: 2022942332

First printing

Contents

Acknowledgments

Many thanks to the Dominican community at École Biblique in Jerusalem for hosting my sabbatical studies for two months. Thanks also to the Diocese of Charleston for providing a refreshing time of sabbatical and to Fr. Richard Ballard and the staff of Our Lady of the Rosary parish in Greenville for holding the fort in my absence.

Thanks to Fr. Chris Landfried, networker extraordinaire, for putting me in touch with important people and places in Jerusalem. Thanks to Abouna Rami at St. Catherine's for a warm welcome to the birthplace of Our Lord and to Loai Ibrahim—excellent guide to Bethlehem and Hebron. Youssef Hilo provided an efficient path through Jordan and assisted our travel and studies in a professional, practical, friendly way.

Thanks to the team at Sophia Institute Press for steering the project through at record pace and special thanks to my wife, Alison, for supporting me and my work with patience, intelligence, and an English sense of humor.

—Fr. Dwight Longenecker

The Secret of the Bethlehem Shepherds

Introduction

Whenever one begins to study the Bible seriously, it is not long before troubles arise. Naturally, most Christians hold to a Sunday-school understanding of the Bible. They simply accept what they received in childhood without giving it much extra thought. This means they accept the Bible stories at face value. The Bible is God's Word, so it must be true, and if it is true, that means it is factually true in the way we assume a history book, a biography, or yesterday's news is true.

Along with the Bible stories, most Christians also accept a large amount of what might be called decoration. The decorations are the extra traditions, legends, and interpretations that have accumulated in and around the Bible stories. These decorations add color and interest to the stories, but they are not part of the Bible itself. An example of such decorations is the story of St. Veronica—the woman who wiped Jesus' brow on His way to Calvary. St. Veronica is not in the Bible. In fact, her name indicates where she came from. *Veronica* means "true icon." In later Church history, when the miraculous image of Christ appeared on a cloth—perhaps the Shroud of Turin or the Veil of Manoppello—people wondered where this "true icon" of Christ came from. So the story of Veronica wiping Jesus' brow came to be told, and now Veronica and her veil are in one of the Stations of the Cross, beloved of Catholics everywhere.

Such decorations are not necessarily bad. They add interest and drama to the Faith and usually prompt genuine devotion. It is not a bad thing, however, to trim away the decorations in order to see the true story for what it really is.

The industry of modern biblical scholarship started in the eighteenth century, when the philosophers of the "Enlightenment" began to question the Sunday-school understanding of the Bible. Hermann Reimarus (1694–1768) was a German philosopher who was the first to look at the Gospels with a critical eye. A long line of scholars followed in his footsteps and his philosophy. Sons of the Enlightenment, they were skeptical of the supernatural and sought to understand Scripture from only a "scientific" and verifiable viewpoint.

The Enlightenment attitude culminated in the scholarship of the twentieth century and up to the present day. The result is that any serious student of the Bible will be met with a body of teaching and a troop of teachers who doubt the supernatural origins of Scripture and the historical basis for the Gospel stories.

It is easy to ignore the findings of the scholars and take refuge in the Sunday-school mentality, but this is a mistake. Although many of the underlying attitudes and assumptions of modernist scholars are destructive and negative, their scholarship has yielded much that is truly enlightening and good. The discerning student reads with an open mind and an open heart and sifts the wheat from the chaff.

Happily, many of the negative conclusions about the historical reliability of the Gospels is falling under the weight of new evidence yielded from advanced archaeology, forensics, textual research, and cultural and linguistic studies. The biblical scholar Margaret Barker comments on the revolutionary nature of recent research: "The impact of the last fifty years of discoveries has been comparable to the impact of the Bible translations on the Reformation. New questions have been raised and old certainties have been challenged."[1]

---

[1] Margaret Barker, *Temple Theology, An Introduction* (London: Society for Promoting Christian Knowledge, 2004), 2.

One of the main thrusts of current scholarship regarding the Gospels is to understand the cultural context of the story of Jesus. What kind of a man was He? What was the culture of His world like? What was ordinary family life like? What was the geography? What were the economic and political motivations? How were people educated? How did they see themselves? What was their worldview? The more we understand the world of the New Testament, the more deeply we will understand the New Testament itself.

Some years ago, I embarked on a personal study of one aspect of the Gospel: the story of the Magi, who traveled to Bethlehem to honor the Christ Child. I recorded my findings in *The Mystery of the Magi: The Quest to Identify the Three Wise Men.* Since then, I have continued to be intrigued by the details of the Christmas story. As I learned more about the Magi, I realized that the Christmas story had accumulated more decoration than any other story in the Gospels.

It is natural that it should do so, since the Christmas story is so beloved. A story that involves animals, angels, a young mother and her baby, and a long journey? It has all the attributes of a great tale—a tale that has room for lots of extra detail and loving elaboration.

In my book on the Magi, I attempted to sift out the decoration and put it to one side in order to see the Magi in a more accurate historical context. Later, it seemed to me that there was scope to do the same for the shepherds and other details in St. Luke's version of Jesus' birth.

Therefore, when I was given the opportunity to take a sabbatical from my work as a parish priest, I thought it would be great to dig more deeply into the context of the Bethlehem shepherds.

The best place to do this would be in Bethlehem itself. I would also need a good library to do some research, so I contacted the administrator of the famous École Biblique et Archéologique in Jerusalem. This school of biblical archaeology is also a Dominican convent. It stands just outside the Damascus Gate leading into the Old City of Jerusalem on the traditional site of the martyrdom of St. Stephen.

The guestmaster wrote back inviting me to live in the monastery, with access to its world-class library of biblical studies, and to share in the cycle of prayer and worship with the Dominican friars. For an avid traveler and bookworm, it was a perfect solution! I also made contact with the pastor of St. Catherine Church, which is adjacent to the Church of the Nativity in Bethlehem, so I was able to visit Bethlehem, tour the shepherd's fields, and interview some present-day Bethlehem shepherds.

I trust this little book will shed light on the Bethlehem shepherds, deepen readers' knowledge, and so strengthen their faith in the Shepherd-King born in Bethlehem two thousand years ago.

Jerusalem
Ascension Day 2022

Chapter 1

The Christmas-Card Shepherds

Ebenezer Scrooge and the Grinch are the only ones who don't love Christmas—but even they came around eventually. The child in all of us gets excited as December arrives and the countdown to Christmas begins. It's a magical time of the year, with sentimental Christmas movies, carols, cards, and snowy scenes warmed by family, good friends, good food, and faith.

When I say Christmas is magical, I do not mean only the magic of good times and good cheer. Christmas has become populated with magical characters: flying reindeer, singing snowmen, and a jolly elf who squeezes down every chimney in the world all in one magical night. And it's not only the make-believe characters who are magical. The characters surrounding the Bible story of Jesus' birth also seem to radiate an aura of magic.

Mary and Joseph, along with the shepherds of Bethlehem and John the Baptist's father, Zechariah, all receive visits from angels. The Wise Men are mystical wizards who follow a magical star across the desert sands. They are called "Magi," from which we get the word *magic*. God speaks to them and to St. Joseph in dreams. The whole story is steeped in what seems to be magical make-believe. Indeed, at the very heart of the story is a marvelous miracle—that God Himself chooses to put on human flesh through the Blessed Virgin Mary and participate in the great drama of human history.

To our scientifically conditioned mindset, these supernatural events—a magical moving star, encounters with angels, messages from Heaven delivered in dreams—seem unreal. We are taught to distrust stories of the supernatural. As a result, whenever there is a supernatural element to a story, too many of us simply dismiss the whole story as being either a pious legend or a lovely parable that is meant to teach a lesson.

This is the approach of the majority of biblical scholars: the Christmas story isn't true in a historical sense; instead, it is a lovely collection of parables that, like Aesop's fables, teach us nice lessons to live by. In other words, St. Luke's Gospel is like an older version of *The Little Drummer Boy*.[2]

---

[2] Marcus J. Borg and John Dominic Crossian, *The First Christmas: What the Gospels Really Teach about Jesus's Birth* (San Francisco: HarperOne, 2007).

The stories retold in the Gospels, however, are not quite as simple as all that. They do contain supernatural elements, but that doesn't mean they are fairy tales. They do teach theological truth and moral lessons, but they do so by relating stories that really happened—stories that are rooted in the lives of real people in real places in human history. My two-month sabbatical in Jerusalem hammered home this very point: these stories are real. This is where it happened. The very stones themselves cry out, "We were here. We are witnesses."[3]

The simple story of the nativity of Jesus Christ is told in two of the four Gospels: Matthew and Luke. Like a wall that has ivy growing over it, however, the story has been added to and elaborated over its two-thousand-year history. As a result, the story that we tell every Christmas is an elaborate version of the bare-bones story told by Matthew and Luke. It is, if you like, not a bare pine tree, but a Christmas tree complete with lights, tinsel, baubles, and a shining star on top.

The decorations attached to the simple stories of Luke and Matthew have come about in various ways and for various reasons. The stories have been elaborated in four ways: tradition, interpretation, legend, and myth. We need to cut away

[3] See Luke 19:40.

the elaboration and look at Luke's and Matthew's stories in their simplicity. Then we will be able to discover the historical and cultural details so we can understand better what really happened at Jesus' birth in Bethlehem two thousand years ago.

Because the stories in Matthew and Luke are so brief, we can use facts we have found in historical research to help fill in the gaps. The evidence comes from ancient texts, from archaeological discoveries, and from real-life experiences of scholars who have lived and worked in the Holy Land for decades. Some of this "filling in the gaps" will be simple common sense. Some will be logical speculation. And some will be imaginative speculation—wondering (considering the lack of information) what might have been.

Tradition

The first disciples of Jesus obviously told others about what they had heard and seen. This is what we refer to as "oral tradition." I will discuss this in more detail in chapter 10, but it is good to understand that the stories of Jesus were first gathered together by His disciples through the process of preaching and sharing the good news orally.

Very soon, however, Jesus' followers began to write down the things He said and did. The next generation spoke to those who had known Jesus and began to collect the stories and sayings in written form. Many scholars believe that the apostle Matthew was the first to collect the sayings and actions of Jesus in the Hebrew or Aramaic language.[4] Matthew collected these sayings and acts from his own memories and from other eyewitness accounts.[5] If this is the case, then the version we now read as Matthew's Gospel was written after the original Hebrew version because it is in Greek. It is possible that this Greek version of Matthew was a later edition by Matthew himself or by another writer in the early apostolic tradition.

Although he wasn't one of the apostles, St. Mark was probably among the number of Jesus' disciples in the Jerusalem area, and we know he was a companion of St. Peter.[6] The Fathers of the early Church report that Mark's Gospel

---

[4] Eusebius, *History of the Church* 3, 39, 14–17. Eusebius was a Church historian from the fourth century who recorded the witness of Papias—a bishop in the second century who was a disciple of St. John and Polycarp.

[5] Richard Bauckham's book *Jesus and the Eyewitnesses* is the best book showing how the Gospels are rooted in eyewitness accounts.

[6] See 1 Peter 5:13.

was based on the preaching and memories of Peter.[7] Mark probably also drew on the memories and traditions that Matthew had collected in Aramaic or Hebrew.

St. Luke was also not an apostle, but he was a companion of St. Paul, and Richard Bauckham points out that if Luke was with Paul when he went to Jerusalem to meet with the apostles,[8] he would have had contact with Jesus' extended family members, who would have shared with him the traditions about Jesus' birth.[9] "The tradition took shape in, and was handed down from the circle of Jesus' extended family."[10]

---

[7] Eusebius, *History of the Church* 3, 39, 15. For a full list of evidence from the apostolic Fathers, see J. Warner Wallace, "Is Mark's Gospel an Early Memoir of the Apostle Peter?" Christianity.com, January 17, 2014, https://www.christianity.com/blogs/j-warner-wallace/is-marks-gospel-an-early-memoir-of-the-apostle-peter.html.

[8] This event took place around the year AD 49 and is mentioned in Acts 15:2 and Gal. 2:1.

[9] Richard Bauckham, "Luke's Infancy Narrative as Oral History," in *The Gospels, History and Christology: The Search of Joseph Ratzinger–Benedict XVI*, ed. Bernardo Estrada, Ermenegildo Manicardi, and Armand Puig i Tàrrech (Citta del Vaticano: Libreria Editrice Vaticana, 2013), 407–408.

[10] R. Reisner, *Matthew and Luke*, in *The Gospels, History and Christology*, 478.

When we read the stories about Jesus' birth in Luke and Matthew, the first thing that strikes us is how different they are. Luke tells us about the angel Gabriel visiting Mary, Mary's visitation to Elizabeth, the birth of John the Baptist, the nativity, the shepherds, the presentation in the Temple, and the finding of the boy Jesus in the Temple. St. Matthew omits all these elements of the story. Instead, he tells us about the Magi, King Herod, the flight into Egypt, and the slaughter of the Innocents. Because they seem to be two different stories, many scholars have concluded that both Matthew's and Luke's accounts are literary constructions added to the Gospels much later in order to boost the supernatural aspect of Jesus' life.

How do we deal with the obvious differences in the stories? Are they contradictory, or is it simply the case that Matthew and Luke are relating different aspects of the same story, but from different perspectives and with different motives? Other problems remain. If Matthew was written first, and Luke knew of Matthew's Gospel, why didn't he refer to the Wise Men and the flight into Egypt?

It could be that Matthew's early collection of Jesus' sayings and actions did not include the stories about His birth and were added later, when the Greek version of Matthew's Gospel was compiled. If that is the case, and the later, Greek version of Matthew was written after Luke's Gospel, why didn't the author of Greek Matthew at least mention the stories that only Luke relates? For example, Luke has Joseph and Mary residing in Nazareth and having to travel to Bethlehem. Matthew seems to think they lived in Bethlehem and only went to Nazareth after they returned from Egypt.

I think the answer lies in the nature of oral tradition. Put simply, the people Luke interviewed about the birth of Jesus remembered certain details, and the people Matthew interviewed remembered others.

With eyewitness accounts, we all understand that what we remember is automatically filtered through our own experiences, expectations, emotions, beliefs and presuppositions. For example, if I remember the birth of my daughter, I may recount not only the date and time of her birth but also my feelings of joy when I first saw her, the details about her Baptism a few days later, how my wife and I chose a name for her and perhaps what the newspapers were reporting that day.

My story about my daughter's birth will naturally be limited in detail and perspective. My wife's or my mother-in-law's memories of the same event will be from a different perspective, and either one's account might seem like a very different event—one that in no way resembles my account.

Likewise, the witnesses who spoke to Matthew and Luke (were they actually St. Joseph and the Blessed Virgin, as many have supposed?) will have shared their memories, filtered through their own experiences, and those, over the years, may well have developed. Certain details became more important and meaningful. Others faded in importance until they were eventually forgotten.

These oral traditions form the basis of the stories in Matthew's and Luke's Gospels, but very early on, these stories were augmented by another layer of tradition. This second generation of tradition consists of what are called "apocryphal gospels," written in the first three or four centuries.

Some of the apocryphal gospels may have historical details embedded in them, but because they were written so long after the events, they are more likely to be corrupted by the authors' ignorance and infected with fanciful notions and a theological agenda. The apocryphal gospels are notoriously unreliable even if they do echo some historical details.

In the early centuries of the Church, before the official list of biblical books was decided, the apocryphal gospels were often included in the liturgy and trusted as historical sources. Many of the details from the apocryphal gospels became part of the Church's shared memory and tradition about the Christmas story. An example of this is the tradition that Mary rode a donkey from Nazareth to Bethlehem. Matthew and Luke do not mention a donkey. However, the apocryphal gospel of James—often referred to as the *Protoevangelium of James*—includes the detail of Mary riding a donkey to Bethlehem.

It is possible, and, in fact, perfectly probable, that the pregnant Mary rode a donkey to Bethlehem, but this is part of the ancient nonbiblical tradition. It is not a detail we find in Matthew or Luke. The fact that Mary and her donkey have found their way into the magic of Christmas shows how the traditions have added decoration to the simple story.

Interpretation

In addition to the accumulated traditions, the historical story of Jesus' birth was elaborated by theological interpretation. This interpretation of events began with Matthew and Luke, continued into the writings and preaching of the early Church, and has continued for the last two thousand years. Preachers read their own theology and their own current issues into the stories told by Matthew and Luke.

Interpretation of the events is clear in Matthew and Luke because both evangelists are obviously telling the story to show that Jesus of Nazareth is the Messiah, the Son of David, the Son of God, our Savior. Matthew and Luke show how the details of Jesus' birth fulfill Old Testament prophecies. Their interpretations of the events color the way they tell their stories and help them decide which details to include. So, for example, they tell us about Bethlehem, the city of David, in order to reveal that Jesus is the Son of David.

Later preachers and teachers interpret the story further, and in so doing, they add details to the story. For example, they see in the story of Jesus' birth a fulfillment of Isaiah 1:3, "The ox knows its owner, and the ass its master's crib; but Israel does not know, my people does not understand." Because they connect this verse with Jesus' birth, the ox and the ass make their entrance into the Christmas story. In fact, as British scholar Margaret Barker has discovered, "The ox and ass do not appear in a nativity text until the *Gospel of Pseudo-Matthew* compiled perhaps in the eighth century."[11]

---

[11] Margaret Barker, *Christmas: The Original Story* (London: Society for Promoting Christian Knowledge, 2018), 77. Note: The gospel of Pseudo-Matthew is one of many "apocryphal" gospels written much later than the Gospels themselves that elaborate on the Gospel stories and are written by anonymous authors who assumed the names of the apostles to give their writings added authority.

Matthew and Luke don't mention an ox or an ass in the Christmas scene. Later interpretations add that detail.

An example of modern interpretation becoming part of the story is the idea that Mary and Joseph were homeless people. We'll see later how this is untrue. Nevertheless, it is an easy mistake to make, and because it fits in with our Christian compassion for refugees and the homeless, it has become part of the larger Christmas story.

Legend

Along with the additions of tradition and interpretation, the Christmas story is elaborated by legendary elements. In *The Lord of the Rings*, Galadriel says, "History became legend, and legend became myth." Legend is the further elaboration of history over time. An example of legend is the story of King Arthur. Historians believe there was a real British chieftain named Arthur, but the stories told about him soon grew over time and became legends. The legends engendered poems, novels, and even Broadway musicals and Disney films, so more legendary and elaborations accumulated. The legends were rooted in real events, but they morphed into fantasy.

Legendary elements also attached themselves to the stories of Jesus' birth. The legends came about as the stories were retold in different historical and cultural contexts. They then became part of the generally accepted story that was passed down to further generations.

An example of a legendary aspect of the Christmas story is the rustic nativity scene in a rundown cattle shed that gives all of us our much-loved nativity scene. This aspect of the Christmas story comes to us from St. Francis in thirteenth-century Italy.

Wanting to make the Christmas story more relatable to the people of his age, St. Francis set up a Christmas crèche. He naturally assumed that the stable where Jesus was born was similar to the barnlike stable of his day. As we will see, the stable in Bethlehem was very different, but the "lowly cattle shed" we all take for granted was a legendary element that was added to the story much later.

Myth

We should not be disturbed by the word *myth* when talking about the Gospels. By *myth*, most people mean a fairy tale – a made-up, untrue story. A better understanding of *myth*, however, is "a story with multiple levels of meaning." The story itself could be either pure fiction or the narrative of a historical event. The Gospels are mythical inasmuch as multiple levels of meaning are embedded in historical stories. In addition to the historical level of meaning, there is a moral level, a theological level, and an allegorical level.

Sometimes the theological or moral levels of meaning have prevailed over the historical, and because preachers and teachers wish to emphasize the deeper levels of the story, this process has added more decoration or elaboration to the story.

A good example of this process has to do with the swaddling cloths. Some preachers suggest that the Baby was wrapped in swaddling cloths and born in a cave because it was a tragic pointer to the fact that one day that Baby would be wrapped in a linen shroud and laid in a cave after His death. This is a nice preaching point, but to add it to the Christmas story is to add a level of meaning and myth. There is nothing wrong with this *per se*, but we should be aware that this is an elaboration on the story—not a part of Matthew's and Luke's accounts.

The infancy stories have accumulated more elements of tradition, interpretation, legend, and myth than any other parts of the Gospel. Because of this, many scholars have rejected the stories of Jesus' birth as total fictions—fanciful tales invented by Luke and Matthew to make Jesus more of a supernatural hero. Most of what they are rejecting are the levels of tradition, interpretation, legend, and myth that have become attached to the basic stories.

If we sift out these extra levels, we should be able to uncover the simple tale that is told by Matthew and Luke and thereby enrich our understanding and experience of Christmas.

Chapter 2

Mary and Joseph

The story doesn't begin in Bethlehem. As we all know, it begins in the Galilean village of Nazareth—about ninety miles north of Bethlehem. Although Mary and Joseph's Christmas journey began in Nazareth, I believe their story has its real beginnings in Judea, the southern part of Israel, with Jerusalem as its capital.

I have come to this conclusion because of certain questions that arise when we read the Christmas story in Luke's and Matthew's Gospels.

The Christmas story, as we tell it year after year, is simple: Mary and Joseph were living in Nazareth and were engaged to be married. Then the emperor decreed that everyone had to be registered for taxation purposes in his hometown.[12]

[12] There seems to be a historical mistake at the beginning of Luke's account of the birth of Christ. The census, Luke says, took place "while Quirinius was governor," but this doesn't connect with the historical details we have about

Because Joseph was from Bethlehem, he loaded heavily pregnant Mary onto a donkey and made the journey to Bethlehem, where the Baby Jesus was born in a stable because there was no room for them in the inn.

When we examine the Gospel accounts more closely and compare them with the earliest Church traditions, some puzzling questions arise.

First of all, we are confronted with the question of locations. Nazareth is in Galilee, the northern part of Israel. Bethlehem is near Jerusalem, a four-day journey to the south.[13] Bethlehem is Joseph's hometown, and Church tradition says Mary was born in Jerusalem.[14]

Roman censuses and Quirinius. Scholars have debated endlessly about this conundrum. The solution is simple: either Luke made a human error, or we don't have enough information about events so long ago and so far away. It is more likely the latter since Luke's history in other places is pretty impressive.

[13] S. Safrai and M. Stern in cooperation with D. Flusser and W. C. van Unnik, *The Jewish People in the First Century: Historical Geography, Political History, Social, Cultural, and Religious Life and Institutions* (Assen: Van Gorcum, 1974), vol. 2, 686.

[14] The apocryphal *Protoevangelium of James* says Mary's childhood home was in Jerusalem near the Temple. The

If this is the case, why were Joseph and Mary living in Nazareth? Some scholars say Luke placed them in Nazareth to comply with Jesus' title as "the Nazarene" but that they really lived in Bethlehem.[15] Others have suggested that conservative Jews from Judea who were sympathetic to the spirituality of the monastic-style Essene sect migrated north to settle in Galilee.[16] Joseph and Mary may also have moved to Galilee for economic reasons. There were good job opportunities in the growing Galilean cities of Sepphoris and Tiberias. Joseph, as a carpenter and builder, may well have been drawn north to Galilee from his hometown of Bethlehem for employment.

If this is so, we have Mary, who must have been a young teenager,[17] living in Nazareth while engaged to Joseph. The rules for the betrothal period in Galilee were stricter than in

---

traditional site can be visited today near the Church of St. Anne, by the Lion's Gate.

[15] Raymond E. Brown, *The Birth of the Messiah: A Commentary on the Infancy Narratives of Matthew and Luke* (New York: Doubleday, 1993), 396.

[16] Josephus says the Essenes were present in many towns in Palestine. Barker, *Christmas*, 122.

[17] Girls would be betrothed for marriage around the age of twelve or thirteen. Brown, *The Birth of the Messiah*, 123.

Judea,[18] so Mary did not yet share a home with Joseph. If she was from Jerusalem and Joseph from nearby Bethlehem, with whom did Mary live in Nazareth? Some believe Mary was an orphan by this time,[19] and there is an ancient tradition that, as a girl, she had been dedicated to serve in the Temple, a bit like the boy Samuel in the Old Testament.[20] The idea is that she belonged to a sort of girls' convent school, helping with the weaving and textile work necessary for Temple worship. Once she was of marriageable age, the temple elders chose a husband for her.[21]

While we can't be sure of the details, we can speculate to fill in the blanks: Joseph, whose hometown is Bethlehem,

---

[18] Brown, *The Birth of the Messiah*, 124.

[19] There is an ancient Coptic tradition that Mary's father, Joachim, died when Mary was six and St. Anne when Mary was eight. Sr. Danielle Peters, "Holy Land during Mary's Life: In the Footsteps of Mary of Nazareth," University of Dayton, https://udayton.edu/imri/mary/h/holy-land-during-marys-life.php.

[20] See the *Protoevangelium of James*, trans. Alexander Walker, in *Ante-Nicene Fathers*, vol. 8, ed. Alexander Roberts, James Donaldson, and A. Cleveland Coxe (Buffalo: Christian Literature Publishing, 1886), revised and edited for New Advent by Kevin Knight, https://www.newadvent.org/fathers/0847.htm.

[21] Ibid.

lives just five miles from Jerusalem, and as with many pious Jews, his life and relationships are linked with the Temple community in Jerusalem. Did he know the priest Zechariah, the father of John the Baptist? Mary did, because after the angel Gabriel appeared to her in Nazareth, she hurried to visit her kinswoman Elizabeth, Zechariah's wife.

This leads us to wonder what the relationship was between Mary and Elizabeth. St. Luke says Elizabeth was Mary's kinswoman. We are not told more than that. Was Elizabeth Mary's aunt, the sister of St. Anne? If Mary was an orphan, did Zechariah and Elizabeth care for her? Elizabeth and Zechariah were childless. Did they foster or even adopt Mary? If so, was Zechariah instrumental in arranging the betrothal of Joseph and his foster daughter, Mary? The tradition from the *Protoevangelium* suggests that this was the case.

And what about St. Joseph? Was he a young man or an old man? The *Protoevangelium* says he was an older widower and that the "brothers and sisters of Jesus"[22] we read about in the Gospels were Joseph's children from an earlier marriage. Later traditions assert that Joseph was a young man, who, like Mary, remained a virgin. The Church allows for either opinion.

[22] See Mark 6:3; Matt. 13:56.

The answer is, we just don't know. What we do know is that Joseph disappears from the Gospel account after the story of Jesus teaching in the Temple at the age of twelve, and we assume that he died before Jesus' ministry began. This lends weight to the most ancient tradition that he was an older widower.

Joseph and Mary's betrothal and marriage also makes us wonder about the nature of their relationship. Was it normal for an older man to marry a very young woman? Did they really marry but never have marital relations? Did Mary have other children with Joseph? The Church says no, and the doctrine of the perpetual virginity of the Blessed Virgin is a very early tradition. It is fair to wonder, however, "If a marriage is never physically consummated, is it really a marriage?"

St. Paul recommends celibacy within marriage,[23] and there is evidence from the Essene community that celibate marriage for pious Jews was not unheard of.[24] I had an interesting experience that provides evidence for a celibate marriage between an older man and younger woman in Middle Eastern culture. I had heard that there was a custom that

[23] 1 Corinthians 7:5.

[24] Otto Betz, "The Essenes," in *Judaism*, vol. 3, *The Early Roman Period*, ed. William Horbury, W. D. Davies, and John Sturdy (Cambridge: Cambridge University Press, 1999), 444.

when a young girl who was an orphan reached the age of puberty, the elders of the community might choose an older, responsible, and respectable man to be betrothed to her as a way of adopting her, so that she might have someone to look after her. He would "marry" the young girl, and she would join his extended family as his betrothed wife. The older girls and women would watch over her to protect her virtue, and when she was older, she would enter the marriage fully.

I was explaining this in an RCIA class that included some members of our local Maronite community from Lebanon. After I explained this custom, one of the Lebanese men said, "Yes, Father. This is true. We still have this custom in the Middle East. The women in the family look after the young girl when she is married to an older man, who must not have relations but must protect her like an uncle."

A celibate marriage seems strange to us, and the marriage between a young girl and an older man might strike us as a bit creepy, but in a different culture and a different time, the marriage between Joseph and Mary would have perfectly acceptable.

If all these pieces fit together, we can imagine the orphaned Mary living among Joseph's extended family in the village of Nazareth in Galilee when she receives the message from the angel Gabriel. On receiving the news and becoming pregnant by the power of the Holy Spirit, she rushes south to the hill country of Judea—just a few miles from Jerusalem—to visit her relative (and possibly her adoptive mother) Elizabeth, with whom she stays for the first three months of her own pregnancy.

Would a young girl of maybe only thirteen years of age set out on a four- or five-day journey on her own from Galilee to the town of Ain Karem, the traditional site of Zechariah and Elizabeth's home, a few miles from Jerusalem? In a fascinating book entitled *Papyri and the Social World of the New Testament*, Sabine Huebner explores the evidence from ancient documents from Egypt. She explains how women traveled especially during times of pregnancy to be with other family members who were expecting—often over very long distances.[25] Usually they traveled with others in a group, and this would align with the evidence in Luke 2:44, where we see Joseph and Mary traveling back from Jerusalem with a caravan of other pilgrims. We can conclude from this evidence that Mary probably joined one of the regular pilgrim caravans headed to Jerusalem from Galilee to visit Elizabeth.

---

[25] Sabine Huebner, *Papyri and the Social World of the New Testament* (Cambridge: Cambridge University Press, 2019), 95-96.

Putting together the pieces of the puzzle, we can see Joseph, a widower whose home was in Bethlehem near Jerusalem, agreeing to be betrothed to Mary, an orphan girl from Jerusalem who was related to the priest Zechariah.

Joseph moves with Mary and his first family to the village of Nazareth to be part of a more committed religious community and to find employment in the growing cities of Galilee. While there, Mary is looked after by the older women of Joseph's extended family, and when she becomes pregnant, Joseph has a dream in which an angel commands him not to be afraid to take Mary as his wife.

Mary joins a caravan headed toward Jerusalem to visit Elizabeth. This not only enables her to visit her kinswoman who, in her old age, is also pregnant, but it reduces the risk of scandal in the conservative, close-knit community back in Nazareth. Notice the detail that Mary is with Elizabeth for the first three months of her pregnancy, but Elizabeth was already six months pregnant at that point. This means Mary travels to visit Elizabeth and remains there for the birth of John the Baptist.

After the birth of John, Mary goes back to Nazareth, and when news comes of the Roman census, Joseph has to return to his family town of Bethlehem, and the journey to Jesus' birth begins.

Chapter 3

O Little Town of Bethlehem

The journey from Nazareth to Bethlehem is about ninety miles. To avoid the hilly and unfriendly territory of Samaria, it was customary for pilgrims from Galilee to take the road that runs North of the Sea of Galilee and follow an easier road southward along the low-lying Jordan valley on the eastern side of the Sea of Galilee. Once they got to Jericho, where the Jordan River flows south from the Sea of Galilee to the Dead Sea, they would turn west to make the steep climb from the lowest place on earth—the Dead Sea—to the heights of Jerusalem, about 2,500 feet above sea level.

Bethlehem is just five miles from Jerusalem and is famous for being the "city of David." In Old Testament times, Bethlehem was a small, fortified city. We know this from the archaeological record and also because, in the Old Testament, David cries out for water "from the well of Bethlehem which is by the gate."[26] David's grandson, King Rehoboam, built up the fortifications of his ancestral city.[27] The town was also famous for being the burial place of Rachel, the wife of the patriarch Jacob.[28] The prophet Micah predicted that from this city would "come forth ... one who is to be ruler in Israel, whose origin is from of old, from ancient days."[29]

By the time of Jesus' birth, however, a thousand years had passed since Bethlehem's fame in the time of King David and King Solomon. By the end of the first century BC, Bethlehem had declined to a small village of farmers and herdsmen.

Some scholars have argued that Jesus was born in another Bethlehem in Galilee, not far from Nazareth, and many assert that he was born in Nazareth, not in Bethlehem. They argue that Matthew's and Luke's accounts of Jesus' birth in Bethlehem were invented to fulfill the Old Testament prophecy in Micah 5:1.[30] It is remarkable that biblical scholars,

[26] 2 Sam. 23:15.
[27] 2 Chron. 11:6.
[28] Gen. 35:19.
[29] Mic. 5:2. In some other versions, this prophecy is in Micah 5:1.
[30] Steve Mason, "Where Was Jesus Born? O Little Town of ... Nazareth?," *Bible Review* 16 no. 1 (February 2000): 31–39.

who are so suspicious of speculation without evidence, are so quick to speculate that Jesus was born in Nazareth when all the evidence points to Bethlehem!

While it is true that Jesus' birth fulfills the prophecy in Micah, famed biblical scholar Jerome Murphy-O'Connor says it is unlikely that Matthew dredged through the Old Testament looking for a prophecy that he could make up a story about. Instead, Matthew knew of the account of Jesus' birth in Bethlehem and realized that it fit the Old Testament prophecy. O'Connor asserts that "an event evoked the prophecy; the prophecy was not the source of the event."[31]

Pope Benedict XVI writes, "The two different strands of tradition agree on the fact that Bethlehem was Jesus' birthplace. If we abide by the sources, it is clear that Jesus was born in Bethlehem and grew up in Nazareth."[32]

Archaeological evidence also points to Bethlehem as the birthplace of Jesus. The Church of the Nativity that stands in Bethlehem today was built in the sixth century by the emperor Justinian on the site of a fourth-century church

[31] Jerome Murphy-O'Connor, "Where Was Jesus Born? Bethlehem … of Course," *Bible Review* 16, no. 1 (February 2000): 43.

[32] Joseph Ratzinger/Pope Benedict XVI, *Jesus of Nazareth: The Infancy Narratives* (New York: Image Books, 2018), 66

built by the emperor Constantine. Why did Constantine choose to build on that site? Because one hundred years after Jesus' death and Resurrection, the emperor Hadrian—in an attempt to stamp out Christian devotions—constructed a pagan temple on the site of a cave that the locals had venerated as the birthplace of Christ.[33] This detail, that the local inhabitants of Bethlehem remembered the location of Christ's nativity, will be an important piece of the puzzle in discovering the secret of the Bethlehem shepherds.

Ironically, this attempt to quash Christianity actually preserved the memory of the exact location in Bethlehem where the locals believed Jesus was born. So, when the emperor Constantine's mother, St. Helena, went looking for the nativity site in the fourth century, it was clear that Jesus was born in that place. Even earlier, around the year 150, Justin Martyr, who was a native of Samaria, reported that Jesus was born in a cave in Bethlehem. This was supported by Origen (d. 253), who visited the site, and St. Jerome (d. 420), who lived next to the cave of Christ's birth for many

---

[33] Hadrian did the same thing in Jerusalem: he buried the site of Jesus' death and Resurrection and built a pagan temple over it. In doing so, he actually preserved the site on which the Church of the Holy Sepulchre now stands.

years.[34] Therefore, anyone who visits the Church of the Nativity in Bethlehem is almost certainly visiting the actual site where Jesus was born.[35]

Our view of "the little town of Bethlehem" is influenced by nineteenth-century Christmas carols, cards, and a romantic vision of a Middle Eastern village with simple houses clustered on a hillside with a star shining over them. But recent scholarship helps us visualize what Bethlehem was like at the time of Jesus' birth.

In *The Jewish People in the First Century*, Hebrew scholar Schmuel Safrai paints a picture of life in a Jewish village in Palestine. The simple, one-roomed houses were grouped around a courtyard where the cooking and socializing took place. The common space of the courtyard might also have

---

[34] Jerome Murphy-O'Connor, *The Holy Land: An Oxford Archeological Guide from Earliest Times to 1700* (Oxford: Oxford University Press, 1998), 200.

[35] The Church of the Nativity is occupied by the Greek Orthodox Church. The Latin (Roman) Catholics occupy the Church of St. Catherine, immediately adjacent to the Church of the Nativity. In the lower, crypt level of St. Catherine's Church, pilgrims can visit the cell of St. Jerome and view the site of his burial. His relics were translated to the Church of St. Mary Major in Rome in the twelfth century.

held various sheds for storage, chicken coops, and dovecotes. The courtyard was enclosed by a wall or fence with a gate that opened onto very narrow streets and alleyways.[36]

Although the houses usually had only one room for the family to live in, there was extra living space on the roof of the house, which was accessed by an exterior staircase. The roof space might had have an arbor for shade and a guest room. In the area around Bethlehem, these simple houses were often built in front of a cave. An archaeological survey near the Church of the Nativity shows that the caves in the area were occupied at the time of Jesus' birth.[37]

Although Bethlehem today is a modern city, when you travel to the Holy Land you can get a glimpse of the simple dwellings that would have made up the village of Bethlehem two thousand years ago. When you travel in Israel and Jordan, you can't miss the Bedouin encampments. Even today, you can see, in the middle of the desert, the tents and the flocks of goats and sheep of these seminomadic tribesmen. Alongside the road are shepherds wandering with their flocks, as the Bedouin people have been doing for centuries. Today's Bedouin culture can give us important

[36] Safrai, *The Jewish People*, vol. 2, 728–730.
[37] Murphy-O'Connor, *The Holy Land*, 99.

information about the life of shepherds in Palestine at the time of Jesus' birth.

In some hilly areas, if you look closely, you will see that Bedouin tents are often erected in front of caves. Professor Murphy-O'Connor points out that "many houses in the area are still built in front of caves."[38] On a visit to Bethlehem, our guide took us to meet a Bedouin shepherd. During our visit, he showed us a cave in the hillside that once housed a family. The cave was still there, but the house that had been built in front of the cave—probably a Bedouin tent or simple lean-to structure—was gone.

During our visit to Bethlehem, we also visited the Church of Our Lady of Fatima in the nearby town of Beit Sahour, the town where the shepherd's fields are located. The pastor, Fr. Issa Hijazeen, showed us caves below his church that archaeologists say were occupied thousands of years ago. The same is true of the caves beneath the Bethlehem Church of St. Catherine, next to the ancient Church of the Nativity.

These hints—still visible two thousand years later—indicate what the village of Bethlehem was like when Jesus was born. It was a mixture of Bedouin tents in front of caves, and simple one-room cave houses nestled on the hillside. The

[38] Ibid.

same type of dwellings had been occupied by the shepherd families in the time of the shepherd boy David and earlier.

A visit to the Shepherd's Fields in Beit Sahour includes a cave where shepherds would have sheltered, and our guide took us to explore a further network of caves in the hillside.

The village of Bethlehem was a small community of farmers and shepherds. Hardly a place for a traveler's hotel or pilgrims' hostel.

Chapter 4

No Room
at the Inn

The typical retelling of the Christmas story has Joseph, Mary, and the donkey arriving in Bethlehem on a cold, winter night, looking for a place to stay. All the hotels have "No Vacancy" signs on display because so many people, like Mary and Joseph, have arrived in Bethlehem to register for the census. A grumpy innkeeper turns Mary and Joseph away but, on second thought, tells them they can shelter in the stables if they want to. By now, Mary is experiencing contractions and desperate for a place where she can give birth. Joseph finds a makeshift shelter in a drafty shed with the donkeys and oxen. He fills a rickety wooden feeding trough with straw to make a crib for the newborn, and when Baby Jesus arrives, He is wrapped tightly in strips of cloth and laid in the manger bed.

Is that how it happened? Yes—and no. In a village as small as Nazareth, it's unlikely that there would be any sort of public hostelry. In her study of life in the ancient world,

Sabine Huebner records that along the official Roman roads, spaced about ten miles apart, there was a network of relay station called *mutationes*. These were way stations for changing horses and pack animals.

Spaced about twenty-five miles apart were *mansiones*. These were guesthouses that offered free accommodation for the officially sanctioned guests who were authorized to use the Roman roads.[39] In addition to the official *mansions*, there were public hostelries. St. Luke uses the Greek word *pandocheion* for this kind of inn in the story of the good Samaritan.[40] As Hueber explains, "These inns, also called *katagōgia* in Greek, were located along the main transport routes and were often found on the outskirts of cities or larger villages. They provided travelers from the lower social strata with cheap, hot meals and basic accommodation. *Pandocheia* were widely viewed as disreputable by ancient authors."[41] She goes on to say that these inns were known for "drunken guests, adulterated wine, brawls, theft and prostitution."[42] Quoting classical authors of the time, she

[39] Huebner, *Papyri*, 88.
[40] Luke 10:34.
[41] Huebner, *Papyri*, 111.
[42] Ibid.

says, "It was not uncommon for a landlord's daughter to sell her body as well as wine and a hot meal to travelers."[43]

Because of Bethlehem's small size, it would not have included a safe and official *mansione*, as such guesthouses were located only on the main Roman roads and were available only to travelers on official imperial business. If Bethlehem did have a more basic hostelry, it would not have been a likely place for St. Joseph, "a righteous man,"[44] to have sought shelter in for his betrothed and pregnant young wife.

Furthermore, Bethlehem was Joseph's hometown. Clan loyalty and generous hospitality are hallmarks of Middle Eastern culture.[45] Clinton Bailey, Kenneth Bailey, and John Davis are all Western scholars who have spent decades living in and among the Bedouin and Palestinian people. They recount detailed experiences of the total clan loyalty along with extravagant hospitality offered to guests. The Bedouin are obliged to offer food and housing even to their mortal enemy should he simply turn up at the front door of their tent. Providing lodging for travelers became one of

---

[43] Ibid.

[44] Matt. 1:19.

[45] Clinton Bailey, *Bedouin Culture in the Bible* (New Haven: Yale University Press, 2018), 63–64.

the characteristic ideals of the Jewish people.[46] Given the Middle East's strong culture of hospitality and loyalty to family members, Joseph would have naturally sought shelter with family, not in some squalid brothel.

Kataluma is the Greek word in Luke's story that is usually translated as "inn" and which has led to the legend of the grumpy innkeeper, the imagined "No vacancy" signs, and therefore the popular myth of the Holy Family being homeless.

New Testament scholar Stephen Carlson has done a detailed word study of *kataluma*.[47] Luke uses it elsewhere when Jesus tells His disciples to find a room to celebrate the Last Supper. He says they will find a *kataluma*. Here it is translated "Upper Room." "It was common to add rooms or small structures to the roofs of houses as it became necessary. The most frequent reason was the expansion of a family. A newly married son customarily brought his wife to live in the family house. The father would set aside a room within the house for the couple or build a marital

[46] Safrai, *The Jewish People*, vol. 2, 762.
[47] Stephen C. Carlson, "The Accommodation of Joseph and Mary in Bethlehem," *New Testament Studies* 56, no. 3 (May 2010): 326-342.

house on the roof."[48] These upper rooms were also reserved as guest rooms.

During my time in the Holy Land, I witnessed these customs. As we traveled through Jordan, I noticed many houses that were incomplete. Exposed columns or steel girders extended upward from the first floor. I asked our Jordanian guide Youssef, "Why all the unfinished houses? Do so many people run out of money before they can complete the building?"

"No!" Youssef explained. "We have a custom here that, when a young man marries, he brings his bride home to live with his family. They build an extra floor to the house to welcome their son and his bride." This custom is also referred to in John 14:2–3, where Jesus says, "In my Father's house are many rooms.... When I go and prepare a place for you, I will come again and will take you to myself, that where I am you may be also." Jesus is referring to the wedding customs of His day.

The wedding custom was that a man would be betrothed to his future bride but not live with her. She would remain with her family, and during the betrothal period, the young man would return to his father's house and build an extra

[48] Safrai, *The Jewish People*, vol. 2, 731.

room to the side or on the roof. The wedding ceremony was completed when he took his bride to live in his father's house.[49]

Stephen Carlson believes that the word *kataluma*, translated as "inn," is really referring to the upper-level guest room or marital chamber that was added to most Palestinian houses. He speculates that Joseph combined his trip to Bethlehem to register with the completion of the second part of his wedding to Mary, by bringing her back to his family home in Bethlehem to dwell in the guest room–cum–bridal suite of his father's house.

The Jesuit biblical scholar Joseph Fitzmyer writes, "It is rather obvious that [*kataluma*] does not mean 'inn'."[50] Kenneth Bailey, another biblical scholar, who lived in the Holy Land for thirty years, also thinks *kataluma* refers to the upper-level guest room: "If Luke expected his readers to think Joseph was turned away from an 'inn,' he would have used the word *pandocheion*, which clearly meant a commercial inn."[51] Bailey points out that the customs of hospitality to

---

[49] Brown, *The Birth of the Messiah*, 124.

[50] Joseph A. Fitzmyer, S.J., *The Gospel according to St Luke* (New York: Doubleday, 1979), 408.

[51] Kenneth E. Bailey, *Jesus through Middle Eastern Eyes: Cultural Studies in the Gospels* (Downers Grove, IL: IVP Academic, 2008), 32.

strangers and the strong family loyalties would most certainly mean that Joseph and Mary were not turned away and made homeless on Christmas night.

Not only did Joseph have family members in Bethlehem, but Mary had her people (Elizabeth and Zechariah) just seven miles away in Ain Karem.[52] Even if Mary's pregnancy was scandalous, according to Bailey, it would have been unthinkable that Joseph's family and Mary's kin would have allowed them to be homeless.

It is far more likely that Joseph, returning to his hometown would have gone to the home either of his father—or, if Joseph was an older man, to the home of a brother or some other member of his extended family. Bailey goes on to explain in more detail what a typical home in Bethlehem would have been like:

Simple village houses had but two rooms. One was exclusively for guests. That room would be attached to the end of the house or be a "prophet's chamber" on the roof. The main room was a family room. At the end of that room, on a lower level was where the animals were kept. Often the lower level would be

[52] Ibid., 28.

a cave—the main room being built in front of the cave. Between the cave and the main room was a stone wall—a half partition where feeding troughs were carved into the stone surface.[53]

A 2009 article in the *Chicago Tribune* reports on Palestinian shepherds who still live in cave houses in the same region. In the article, one of the Bedouin shepherds tells how "the animals live in the lower level and we live in the room above." [54] Bailey concurs: "Such simple homes can be traced from the time of David up to the middle of the twentieth century. I have seen them both in Upper Galilee and in Bethlehem."[55] "Many houses in the area are still built in front of caves and perhaps we should envisage Joseph as taking his wife into such a back area to give birth away from the living room—the cave part would have been used for stabling and storage."[56]

---

[53] Ibid., 29.

[54] Jonathan Broder, "Shepherds' Caves Still Dot the Holy Land," *Chicago* Tribune, December 25, 1987, https://www.chicagotribune.com/news/ct-xpm-1987-12-25-8704050765-story.html.

[55] Bailey, *Jesus through Middle Eastern Eyes*, 29.

[56] Murphy-O'Connor, *The Holy Land*, 200.

So, to put all the evidence together, we can speculate and attempt to build up the picture more accurately. Joseph, who is from Bethlehem, is betrothed to Mary, whose home was in nearby Jerusalem but who may have been fostered by Zechariah and Elizabeth. Zechariah and Elizabeth live in nearby Ain Karem and were members of the priestly fraternity associated with the Temple. Because Mary is an orphan, Joseph adopts her by betrothal and takes her into his extended family. They move to the village of Nazareth, where she lives separately from him—perhaps as a ward of the women of the village. To complete the marriage, Joseph takes her to his family home in Bethlehem both to register for the census and to complete the marriage protocol.

The guest room (*kataluma*) on the roof of his relative's house, however, is either already occupied or is too small and inappropriate as a place for Mary to give birth. So, the couple moves to the warm stable or cave that makes up the back, lower level of the family home. There Jesus is born and is laid in one of the stone feeding troughs in the wall between the stable or cave and the main room of the house. This understanding of the story also connects with Matthew's Gospel, which says the Magi found Mary and the young child in a house rather than in a stable or a cave. These details are also supported by the ancient tradition, first found in the *Protoevangelium of James* and affirmed by Justin Martyr and Origen, that Jesus was born in a cave.[57]

British scholar R. T. France writes, "Jesus was not born in social exclusion, nor in any more squalid a setting than most people regarded as normal living conditions. Not in a cold, droughty, unwelcoming 'stable' but in a warm, if rather crowded, family home. His cradle was unconventional, but not uncomfortable."[58]

In his influential commentary on Luke's Gospel Alfred Plummer writes, "It is a little doubtful whether the familiar translation 'in the inn' is correct.... It is possible that Joseph had relied upon the hospitality of some friend in Bethlehem, whose guest chamber however, was already full when he and Mary arrived."[59]

Kenneth Bailey also quotes William Thompson, a nineteenth-century Presbyterian who observed village homes in Bethlehem: "It is my impression that the birth actually

---

[57] Brown, *The Birth of the Messiah*, 401.

[58] R. T. France, "The Birth of Jesus," in *Handbook for the Study of the Historical Jesus*, vol. 3, ed. Tom Holmén and Stanley E. Porter (Boston: Brill, 2011), 2375.

[59] Rev. Alfred Plummer, *A Critical and Exegetical Commentary on the Gospel according to St. Luke*, 4th ed. (Edinburgh: T&T Clark, 1910), 54.

took place in an ordinary house of some common peasant, and that the baby was laid in one of the mangers such as are still found in the dwellings of farmers in this region."[60]

Some of those farmers were "shepherds keeping watch over their flocks by night."

[60] Bailey, *Jesus through Middle Eastern Eyes*, 31.

Chapter 5

While Shepherds Watched Their Flocks

Like the other aspects of the Christmas story, the account of the shepherds of Bethlehem has attracted charming decorations. The general idea is that the shepherds were a group of country bumpkins who were minding their own business one night when they were interrupted by a wonderful vision of angels who announced the birth of the Messiah.

Rubbing their chins in wonder, they decided to go and see the young child. Over the years, visionaries have told how the shepherds went on to be believers in Jesus and were persecuted for their faith. Beautiful stories were added to the Christmas traditions of the shepherd child who was left behind, or the little drummer boy who had only the gift of playing his drum for the Baby.

In meditating on the Christmas story, I asked myself why the shepherds were so important. St. Luke's account of Jesus' birth is brief. Every element of the story is there not only because it happened but also because it had a deeper meaning. What was the meaning of the shepherds? What was their secret? Why were they so important to St. Luke?

Some scholars suggest that St. Luke added the shepherds to the story he was inventing as a kind of literary flourish. Shepherds appear many times in the legends of Greek religion.[61] The heroes in ancient myths were often raised by simple people such as shepherds, and Greek culture also had a tendency to romanticize the rustic shepherds for being close to nature.[62] In addition to this, "the figure of the shepherd served as a symbolic representation of the ideal ruler not only in ancient Israel, but also across the entire Near East."[63] As John J. Davis notes in his book *The Perfect Shepherd*, "King Hammurabi of Babylon called himself 'the shepherd' as did Abdiheba, King of Jerusalem, along with Shalmaneser, Tukulti-Ninurta and Tiglath-Pileser of Assyria. In Egypt both gods and kings claimed the title of shepherd."[64] Maybe Luke wove in these themes to strengthen Jesus' identity as Israel's Shepherd-King.

[61] Brown, *The Birth of the Messiah*, 420.
[62] I. Howard Marshall, *The Gospel of Luke: A Commentary on the Greek Text* (Exeter, England: Paternoster Press, 1978), 108.
[63] Huebner, *Papyri*, 115.
[64] John J. Davis, *The Perfect Shepherd: Studies in the Twenty-Third Psalm* (Grand Rapids: Baker Book House, 1979), 51.

While these images from the pagan world provide interesting pointers to Jesus the Shepherd-King, the notion that Luke invented the shepherds and their tale in order to give his story extra literary weight and make Jesus more like pagan heroes or ancient monarchs is pure speculation. In his commentary on Luke's Gospel, Norval Geldenhuys concludes, "All attempts made to explain the narrative of the shepherds as an imitation of extra-Biblical stories have failed."[65] Raymond Brown, the expert on the infancy stories, agrees: "It is not plausible ... that such a Semitic story has its primary symbolism derived from pagan mythology."[66]

Instead, we should accept Luke's story as a fairly simple account of what happened. The story in Luke fits perfectly with what we know of the culture and history of the time and of the culture and history of Bethlehem and the Hebron valley.

The shepherds of the ancient Middle East fall into two categories: nomads and seminomads. The nomads are not bound to a particular locality. They are always on the move with their flocks, searching for water and good pastureland.

[65] Norval Geldenhuys, *The Gospel of Luke*, The New International Commentary on the New Testament (Grand Rapids: Eerdmans, 1988), 110.

[66] Brown, *The Birth of the Messiah*, 672.

The ancient Bedouin culture is an example of the nomadic shepherds.

The seminomads belong to settled village communities but "spend a large part of the year outside with their herds moving only between local pastures ... with tents or huts for shelter."[67] The Bethlehem shepherds were of the second category. They tended their flocks in the surroundings of the villages of the Bethlehem area, where they and their ancestors had settled.

Bethlehem was well known as a location for shepherds from David's time and still is today. During our visit to Bethlehem and the West Bank it was common to see small flocks roaming by the roadside with their shepherds. Instead of searching for some obscure literary reason for Luke to have invented the shepherd story, it makes more sense to look at the local culture and history and realize that the hills around Bethlehem were full of shepherds.

The question still arises, however: Why did God choose to announce the birth of His Son to shepherds—and why did Luke consider it so important?

The answer lies in the possibility that these were no ordinary shepherds. Generally speaking, in New Testament

[67] Huebner, *Papyri*, 122–123.

times, shepherds did not have a good reputation. Because their work included contact with feces and blood, the Jewish laws considered them ritually unclean and therefore unable to live righteously.[68] Biblical scholar Walter Liefeld explains that, in the Mishnah, a Jewish collection of rules for life and liturgy, "five lists of proscribed trades are recorded ... and shepherds appear in three of the five." [69] He goes on to say that "shepherds were despised people. They were suspected of not being very careful to distinguish between 'mine' and 'thine.' For this reason, they were barred from giving evidence in court."[70] Sabine Hueber adds that "it was often suspected that shepherds supplemented their income with banditry ... and tax evasion."[71]

Because of this, it is easy to think that Luke included the shepherds simply to echo the Gospel theme that the Messiah has come to the poor, the lowly, and the sinners.[72] This might be part of the reason, but, as usual with the Gospels, there are deeper reasons for the details in the stories, and to

---

[68] Walter Liefeld, *The Expositor's Bible Commentary* (Grand Rapids: Zondervan, 1984), vol. 8, 845.

[69] Bailey, *Jesus through Middle Eastern Eyes*, 35.

[70] Ibid., p. 115.

[71] Huebner, *Papyri*, 132.

[72] Brown, *The Birth of the Messiah*, 673.

understand the deeper reasons, we need more information about the religious and cultural context of the story.

Luke twice mentions that Bethlehem is the city of David and that Joseph is from the "house and lineage of David."[73] King David was famous for being the "shepherd boy of Bethlehem" who not only defended his father's flock from a lion and a bear but also went to battle and defeated the enemy of Israel, the giant Goliath. Bethlehem is, therefore, not only the city of David but also the city of shepherds.

Furthermore, it was prophesied that the Messiah would come from Migdal Eder. *Migdal Eder* means "Tower of the Flock" and is a location near Bethlehem. It is mentioned in two places in the Old Testament. The first is in Genesis, chapter 35. This chapter is important because, in it, Jacob, the grandson of Abraham, is given a new name: Israel; and as God gives him this new name, he makes a promise to Jacob: "A nation and a company of nations shall come from you, and kings shall spring from you."[74] This takes place at Bethel, about ten miles north of Jerusalem. Genesis 35 goes on to tell how Jacob moves on toward Bethlehem, where his wife Rachel dies giving birth to their son Benjamin. Jacob

[73] See Luke 1:27; 2:4.
[74] Gen. 35:11

then settles near Migdal Eder, which is also the traditional location of Rachel's tomb.[75]

At the end of the chapter, Jacob returns to the home of his father, Isaac, in Hebron, about twenty miles away. Isaac dies, and Jacob buries him at Hebron, where you can still visit his tomb.

The Bethlehem area, therefore, is steeped in the history of the Jewish people, who, from the beginning, were shepherds. The area is not only the city of David the shepherd but the area where Abraham, Isaac, and Jacob—also nomadic shepherds—came to settle.

The second place Migdal Eder is mentioned is in Micah 4:8:

> And you, O tower of the flock,
> hill of the daughter of Zion,
> to you shall it come,
> the former dominion shall come,
> the kingdom of the daughter of Jerusalem.

It was in the Bethlehem area that God promised Jacob that a king would come from his family line, and the prophet Micah re-echoes the promise that a king will come from

[75] See Gen. 35:21.

Migdal Eder (Bethlehem). This prophecy in Micah reminds us of the more famous Micah prophecy, quoted in Matthew's Gospel, about a shepherd king from Bethlehem:

> But you, O Bethlehem Ephrathah,
> who are little to be among the clans of Judah,
> from you shall come forth for me
> one who is to be ruler in Israel.

By bringing in the shepherds, Luke also shows us the principle of recapitulation. This is the principle, first outlined by the early Church theologian Irenaeus, that Jesus' life, ministry, death, and Resurrection do not simply fulfill particular detailed prophecies of the Old Testament but that His life gathers up the *whole* of the Old Testament and completes it. In other words, by including the shepherds of Bethlehem in the story, Luke is telling us in symbolic form that *all* the shepherds of the Old Testament and all references to shepherds reach a climax and fulfillment by coming to adore the Christ Child.

In this context, the contemporary scorn for the lowly shepherds is superseded by a great respect and honor for shepherds. New Testament scholar François Bovon concludes, "The rabbinic texts critical of shepherds are not weighty enough to cancel out the positive evaluation of shepherds in Biblical literature. Israel understood themselves as a nation of shepherds."[76]

Father Abraham was a herdsman. Moses was a shepherd after he fled from Egypt. King David was a shepherd, and tradition has it that he wrote the famous Psalm 23: "The Lord Is My Shepherd." The prophet Ezekiel also likens the Lord God to a shepherd, and Israel is referred to repeatedly as his flock. The prophet Amos was a shepherd who lived and worked near Bethlehem. All of these shepherds and prophecies about shepherds are fulfilled and brought to completion as the shepherds of Bethlehem are called to worship the Child who will grow up to say, "I am the good shepherd."[77]

If Jesus is the Good Shepherd, He is also the King of Kings. The ancient image of the shepherd-king, present in both the history of Israel and in pagan cultures, helps to unlock the secret of the Bethlehem shepherds. As shepherds in the city of David, they look back to David the shepherd-king of Israel and look forward to Jesus the Shepherd-King of the universe.

[76] François Bovon, *Luke 1: A Commentary on the Gospel of Luke 1:1-9:50*, trans. Christine M. Thomas, ed. Helmut Koester (Minneapolis: Fortress Press, 2002), 86.

[77] John 10:11.

When He claims the title of the Good Shepherd, Jesus also says, "I know my own [sheep] and my own know me, as the Father knows me and I know the Father; and I lay down my life for the sheep."[78]

That the Good Shepherd-King lays down His life for the sheep brings in another, deeper dimension to the Bethlehem shepherds: the fact that Jesus was not only the Good Shepherd-King but also the Lamb of God. Lambs were the primary animals used for sacrifice in the Temple, and so the Bethlehem shepherds are important not only because they recapitulate and gather up all the shepherds of the Old Testament but because they breed and raise the lambs of God, the sacrifices to be offered in the Temple.

[78] John 10:14–15.

Chapter 6

Behold the
Lamb of God

At Jesus' baptism John the Baptist says, "Behold, the Lamb of God, who takes away the sin of the world!"[79] As we sing in the great hymn "Alleluia! Sing to Jesus," He is "both priest and victim": the Good Shepherd and "the Lamb that was slain."[80]

The shepherds of Bethlehem are not the only ones who are important in the story. The sheep are important as well because it is from the flock that the lambs are taken for the sacrifices offered in the Temple. It is worth taking some time, therefore, to learn more about the Temple sacrifices.

The historian Josephus tells us that at Passover, the multitude of worshippers at the Temple in Jerusalem amounted to as many as 2,700,000, not counting women

[79] John 1:29.
[80] Rev. 13:8.

and children.[81] At the Passover, every household or small grouping of people needed to sacrifice a lamb or a young goat. To fulfill this requirement, Josephus records that, at Passover, 256,500 sheep were slaughtered in the Jerusalem Temple.[82] When you consider that, according to the rubrics, the sacrifices had to take place within a time span of two hours, the numbers seem extraordinarily high. Josephus was notorious for exaggerating his statistics, but even one-tenth of his estimated number means there were over 25,000 sheep sacrificed in one afternoon. And according to the rubrics, the lambs not only had to be slaughtered: they also had to be skinned and butchered, to be ready for roasting.

Whatever the real number, we can certainly conclude that thousands of lambs were needed for the feast of Passover. In addition there was the daily sacrifice called the Tamid service. This was the sacrifice of a lamb in the morning and evening every day. In addition to that would be the regular offerings

[81] Martin Goodman, "The Temple in First Century CE Judaism," in *Temple and Worship in Biblical Israel*, ed. John Day (London: T&T Clark, 2005), 462.

[82] *The New Complete Works of Josephus*, trans. William Whiston (Grand Rapids: Kregel, 1999), 906.

of animals by individuals for various purposes: forgiveness, reconciliation, expiation of guilt, and thanksgiving. Where did all the animals come from?

As Michal Hunt explains, the procedures and protocols for the sacrifices in the Temple were extremely complex.[83] The animals were inspected numerous times. The lambs allocated for sacrifice had to be no more than one year old and had to be free of every blemish.[84] To make sure the animals were worthy, the Temple authorities kept a supply of oxen, sheep, goats, and pigeons that could be purchased in the huge Temple forecourt.[85] Roman money was not allowed in the temple precinct because the coins bore the graven image of the emperor. Therefore, worshippers had to change their money into official Temple currency in order to buy the approved animals for sacrifice. The money changers made a tidy profit on the currency exchange, and the Temple authorities cashed in on the sale of animals. This

[83] Michal E. Hunt, *Jesus and the Mystery of the Tamid Sacrifice* (self-pub., 2020).

[84] Alfred Edersheim, *The Temple, Its Ministry and Services as They Were at the Time of Jesus Christ* (London: Religious Tract Society, 1903), 110.

[85] Ibid.

is the corruption that Jesus famously cleaned up when He cleansed the Temple.[86]

If the Temple authorities had a steady business selling pure, unblemished sacrificial animals, they would have needed reliable suppliers. Who supplied all the animals for the voracious demand of the Temple worship? New Testament scholar R. T. France suggests an answer: "Shepherds in the area around Bethlehem were likely to be raising the sheep needed for the temple sacrifices."[87]

While it is difficult to find concrete evidence of this, there are some very intriguing hints. The Mishnah is a collection of writings by Jewish rabbis detailing the rules of life and worship for the Jewish people. "In Mishnah *Shekalim* 7:4 we are told that animals found between Jerusalem and Migdal Eder were used for temple sacrifice, and this tradition has been used as support for the idea that Luke's shepherds in the region near Bethlehem were especially sacred shepherds."[88] This detail is also pointed out by Alfred Edersheim and Alfred Plummer.[89]

[86] Matt. 21:12–13; Mark 11:15–18; Luke 19:45–46; John 2:13–17.

[87] France, "The Birth of Jesus," 2377.

[88] Brown, *The Birth of the Messiah*, 421.

[89] Plummer, *Gospel according to St. Luke*, 54.

Meanwhile Eberhard Nestle connects this detail with Micah 4:8, which prophesies that the Messiah will come from Migdal Eder, the "Tower of the Flock," otherwise known as the "Watchtower of the Flock." This could be taken to mean not only that the Messiah King will come from the area of Bethlehem but that He will come from the shepherds who were "keeping watch over their flocks" by night.

Were the Bethlehem shepherds breeding and raising the lambs for sacrifice in the Temple? If so, the prophecies indicate not only that the Son of David, the Good Shepherd, would come from Bethlehem but that Bethlehem would also be the origin of the Lamb of God who takes away the sin of the world.

The only time shepherds stay out in the fields all night keeping watch is during the lambing season. So, on the night Jesus was born, the shepherds were probably also assisting in the birth of lambs, some of which would have been destined for the sacrificial rites in the Temple, just five miles away in Jerusalem.

By the way, the fact that shepherds are in the fields all night during lambing season has sometimes been used as evidence that Jesus was born in the springtime. It is true that European breeds of sheep give birth in the spring, so a reader in Europe would draw that conclusion. The breed of sheep indigenous to the Middle East, however, is the Awassi,[90] which usually give birth in November to January, thus providing evidence for the traditional time of Jesus' birth in mid-December.

What was "the Lamb of God" that John the Baptist referred to when he called Jesus "the Lamb of God, who takes away the sins of the world"?[91] What would the Bethlehem shepherds, as faithful Jews, have understood this phrase to mean? Biblical scholar Mary Coloe believes the connection is to the Tamid sacrifice. She writes, "During the time when the Temple of Jerusalem was still standing, one lamb was regularly sacrificed as an offering for the forgiveness of sin. This was the daily burnt offering of the Tamid (continual) liturgy."[92] According to the book of Numbers, this twice daily offering was commanded in the time of the Exodus. "So important was the Tamid offering," Coloe continues, "that

---

[90] H. Epstein, "Awassi Sheep," Food and Agricultural Organization of the United Nations, https://www.fao.org/3/p8550e/P8550E01.htm.

[91] John 1:29.

[92] Mary L. Coloe, "'Behold the Lamb of God': John 1:29 and the Tamid Service," in *Rediscovering John: Essays on the Fourth Gospel in Honor of Frédéric Manns*, ed. L. Daniel Chrupcala (Milan: Edizioni Terra Santa, 2013), 338.

even during the Roman siege of Jerusalem, in the midst of great famine the priests managed to continue this service."[93] The Jewish laws of ritual taught that the Tamid offering was a daily offering for the forgiveness of sins—not just of an individual but also of all the people.

In one of the chapters of the Mishnah, the Tamid sacrifice is described in great detail.[94] Coloe discovers fascinating details that connect the Tamid sacrifice to the death of Jesus as recorded in John's Gospel. Although the legs of the two thieves who were crucified with Jesus were broken to hasten their death, Jesus' legs were not broken. Instead, Jesus' side was pierced with the centurion's lance.[95] This echoes the rules for the sacrifice of the Tamid lamb, whose legs were not broken and whose breast was pierced.[96]

[93] Ibid., 340.

[94] It should be noted that the Mishnah is a collection of teachings and instructions by Jewish rabbis that date a couple of centuries after the time of Christ. This particular chapter on the Tamid offering, however, is considered to be based on the actual activities in the Temple at the time of Jesus. See Louis Ginzberg, "Tamid: The Oldest Treatise of the Mishnah," in *Journal of Jewish Lore and Philosophy* 1 (1919).

[95] John 19:32–36.

[96] Tamid 4:2–3.

We can ask not only, "Why were the shepherds so important to Luke's Gospel?" but also "Why was the birth of a child so important to the shepherds?" Why was this birth so memorable for them? It is not only because "in the city of David" a Savior is born—the Son of the shepherd-king David—but also because that Savior was also destined to be "the Lamb of God, who takes away the sins of the world."

Because they were raising the lambs for the altar, the shepherds had eyes to see that the Child born into an ordinary home like one of theirs was not only the Shepherd-King but also the newborn Lamb of God, and it was the message from the angels that opened their eyes to the truth that this seemingly ordinary Infant was truly extraordinary.

Chapter 7

Angels We Have Heard on High

What I find most interesting about the appearance of the angels to the shepherds is their message and their song, because the angels' message and song unlock the secret of why the shepherds were important to St. Luke.

The angels' message is "Be not afraid; for behold, I bring you good news of a great joy which will come to all the people; for to you is born this day in the city of David a Savior, who is Christ the Lord. And this will be a sign for you: you will find a babe wrapped in swaddling cloths and lying in a manger."[97]

The angels' song is "Glory to God in the highest, / and on earth peace among men with whom he is pleased."[98]

This combination of a message and a song echoes the other angelic appearances in the stories about Jesus' birth. The "angel of the Lord" appears to Zechariah and prophesies

[97] Luke 2:10–12.
[98] Luke 2:14.

John the Baptist's birth. The story is told in the first chapter of Luke's Gospel, and after the message and the birth comes the Song of Zechariah.[99] In the same chapter, the angel Gabriel appears to the Virgin Mary, and after the angelic message comes Mary's song, the Magnificat.[100]

This method of storytelling has its roots in the Old Testament and most often accompanies a supernatural intervention. After some great action of the Lord, the story is recounted in the form of both prose storytelling and an accompanying version in the form of a hymn or poem. So when the Israelites are delivered from slavery in Egypt by crossing the Red Sea, the story of their salvation is related, and Moses and his sister Miriam echo the story with a song of praise.[101]

Likewise, when the Lord gives the judge Deborah victory over Israel's enemy Sisera, Deborah retells the story in a song of praise.[102] When Samuel's mother, Hannah, has her prayer for a son answered, she echoes the story with her song of thanksgiving.[103] This pattern is completed in the story of Jesus' birth when Mary and Joseph take the Child

[99] Luke 1:68–79.
[100] Luke 1:46–55.
[101] Exod. 15:1–19.
[102] Judg. 5.
[103] 1 Sam. 2:1–10.

to be presented in the Temple. There they meet the holy old man Simeon and Anna the prophetess. After they see the child, the event is remembered in Simeon's song, the Nunc Dimittis: "Lord, now lettest thou thy servant depart in peace, according to thy word ..."[104]

Why are the poem songs following the story of God's intervention important? Because they help us understand how people in ancient societies passed on the important events to the next generation.

Narrative poetry is evident as a primary mode of storytelling in most ancient civilizations. The younger generation memorize the stories that retell the important history of their people in the form of narrative poetry.

Clinton Bailey is an American scholar who has lived and worked among the Bedouin people in the land of Palestine for more than forty years. In his book *Bedouin Culture and the Bible*, he tracks hundreds of similarities between the culture of the Bedouin tribes and the Hebrew religion and customs recorded in the Old Testament.

To understand how important his work is, we need to understand the antiquity of the Bedouin culture. Although present-day Bedouin are mostly Muslims, their lifestyle is

[104] Luke 2:29–32.

more than seven thousand years old. Their way of life is rooted in the religion and customs of the nomadic tribes who lived in the ancient Middle East from Old Testament times. The way they live today as nomadic and seminomadic shepherds is largely unchanged from the time of the biblical patriarchs. Put simply, Clinton Bailey shows how Bedouin culture parallels what we know of early Hebrew culture. The Jewish people emerged from the same roots as the Bedouin, and their family likeness continued right through to New Testament times.

Bailey records how the Bedouin use memorized genealogies, proverbs, and poetry to pass on their traditions and history. Memorization is important when most of the population are illiterate. The memorized genealogies, proverbs, and poems are balanced with more expansive prose storytelling. The Bedouin are especially interested in passing on stories of exceptional events — the heroism and cleverness of one of their patriarchs or a supernatural event that transformed the life and culture.

If we want to get a picture of a Bethlehem shepherd, it is not an Englishman dressed in tweeds with his sheepdog on a mountainside in Yorkshire. It is a Bedouin herdsman living in a tent or a cave house in the unforgiving climate and countryside of Palestine, Jordan, Syria, or Western Arabia.

The vision and message of the angels would have been passed down from generation to generation of shepherds, and the combination of genealogies, narrative poems, and storytelling in the infancy narratives shows that they were initially part of the folklore of the local herdsmen.

The angel's message to the shepherds and their song of praise fits the picture of God's interaction with the Hebrew people down through history, and the angels' song of praise is complemented by the message announcing the Messiah's birth—a message that is accompanied by a mysterious sign.

Chapter 8

This Shall Be a Sign unto You

We now come to one of the most puzzling details of Luke's Christmas story: the appearance and announcement of the angel of the Lord to the shepherds: "This will be a sign for you: you will find a babe wrapped in swaddling cloths and lying in a manger."

Why is this puzzling? It is the word *sign*. What is a sign in the Bible? The word is used in several ways. It could be simply an indication of a truth or a direction to walk in. It could be a visual affirmation of a previous statement. So, for example, if I say I love my wife, then a sign of that love is that I embrace her. A sign might also be a visual indication of a mysterious identity. St. John the Evangelist calls Jesus' miracles "signs." These signs confirm Jesus's identity as the Son of God.

Finally, a sign can be a visual affirmation or illustration of a more mysterious pronouncement—a visual revelation of a deeper truth. This is the way Luke uses *sign* here because the first part of the angel's message is this: "To you is born this day in the city of David a Savior, who is Christ the Lord." The angel then goes on to say that the Babe wrapped in swaddling cloths and lying in a manger will be a sign. The angel announces the birth of the Savior in the city of King David, and this Savior is the Messiah, the Anointed One who is to come, the Lord Himself. Therefore, the sign will confirm the message that the Lord, the King, has come. The sign will confirm His identity, but it will also reveal a mysterious truth about His identity.

A legend has developed that, when lambs were born to the Temple flocks, the shepherds would wrap them in strips of cloth to keep them from any harm or blemish and would lay them in a stone feeding trough until the priest could come to inspect them. Thus, the sign to the shepherds was that the long-awaited Lamb of God had been born and that they would find Him (like their own newborn lambs) wrapped in swaddling cloths and lying in a manger.

To me, this seemed too neat to be true. It sounded like a clever preaching point, so I set out to see if there was any truth to the legend. I did not find any evidence for this lovely idea. Furthermore, when I consulted a Jewish scholar from the Hebrew University he said the term "Lamb of God" was not a commonly used term to refer to either the Passover lambs or the other sacrificial animals.

It does seem that the shepherds would sometimes nurture the little lambs like their own young. They would perform the delivery and swaddle the newborn lambs in the folds of their robes.[105] It is also true that that the newborn lambs would be sheltered in the tents or cave homes of the shepherds. A website about the Awassi breed of sheep outlines their birth and nurture: "During the lambing season, lambs born in the field and still too weak to follow their dams are carried by the shepherds to the tents or villages where they remain for a few days until strong enough to join their dams at pasture."[106] The parable about the poor man and his lamb that the prophet Nathan tells King David also reveals an affectionate relationship between shepherd and the lamb.[107]

These details indicate the tenderness with which the shepherds would treat newborn lambs. It might even allow one to speculate that a delicate lamb could be swaddled and taken home to be laid in a manger. But we can't really conclude that the Bethlehem shepherds routinely swaddled the lambs and placed them in mangers. The sign the angels spoke about must have been something else.

[105] Huebner, *Papyri*, 128.
[106] Epstein, "Awassi Sheep."
[107] See 2 Samuel 12.

Why was the "babe wrapped in swaddling cloths and lying in a manger" so important as a sign? The swaddling cloths and the manger must be important because Luke mentions the manger three times and the swaddling cloths twice.

Scholars who like to trace hints of the Old Testament in the New point out that the manger is a fulfillment of Isaiah 1:3: "The ox knows its owner, and the ass its master's crib; but Israel does not know, my people does not understand." The ox and the ass recognize their home, their master, and their feeding trough, but the people of Israel are alienated from the Lord. The prophet wants the people to know and recognize the Lord as instinctively as the family animals know their master and their home.

The sign of the manger, therefore, is the place where the shepherds will find the Lord.

Two more Old Testament verses might shed light on the mystery of the Holy Family's temporary lodging and the swaddling cloths. Jeremiah 14:8 reads as a cry out to the Lord, the Savior: "Why shouldst thou be like a stranger in the land, like a wayfarer who turns aside to tarry for a night?" And Wisdom 7:4 reads, "I was nursed with care in swaddling cloths. For no king has had a different beginning of existence."

In other words, the Lord will be recognized because He is a traveler living in a guest room, and His swaddling cloths will indicate that, although He is a King, He is an ordinary mortal like any other baby.

Clever biblical scholars may have mined the Old Testament to find connections to the manger, the inn, and the swaddling cloths, but did Luke include these details as intentional allusions to the Old Testament prophecies? Furthermore, did the simple shepherds know of the obscure references to Isaiah, Jeremiah, and the Wisdom of Solomon? I doubt it. I think the sign of the manger, the inn, and the swaddling cloths indicate a far simpler and profound truth—a mysterious truth that surprised the shepherds.

For us, the manger bed is important because it is a sign of what we see as Jesus' birth in the lowliest of places—a cold, smelly old stable! As we have seen, however, a manger bed in a first-century cave house in Bethlehem would not have been unusual. If the manger for the animals was a hollowed-out cavity on a half wall between the main room of the house and the back stable room, then it could naturally have doubled as a baby's crib. For us, a manger bed is unusual. For the shepherds, it may have been typical. Likewise, we think of swaddling cloths as whatever rags are handy to wrap a baby in, but swaddling a baby in strips of cloth is the normal custom, not only in the Middle East but in many cultures around the world.[108]

When we visited a Bedouin shepherd near Bethlehem, I asked him how they treated the newborn lambs. He said they would sometimes take them indoors if necessary. "Do you ever wrap them up in strips of cloth?" I asked.

"No" he said, "But we do that for our babies." Therefore, the sign of the child in the manger of Bethlehem is an affirmation to the shepherds that he is not only the heir of the shepherd-king David, but he is also one of them—born into the home of one of their own villagers. He is not wrapped in luxurious furs, silk, or fine fabrics, but he is wrapped in swaddling cloths, as they would wrap their own babies, and is lying in a manger—a place they would also have used as a handy cradle for a newborn.[109]

So the message of the angel, combined with the signs of the manger, the inn, and the swaddling cloths reveal that Jesus is born in the city of His ancestor King David, the place

[108] Ralph Frenken, "Psychology and History of Swaddling, Part Two: The Abolishment of Swaddling from the 16th Century until Today," *Journal of Psychohistory* 39, no. 3 (Winter 2012): 219-245.

[109] M. Bailey, "The Shepherds and the Sign of a Child in the Manger," *Irish Theological Quarterly* 31 (1964): 1-23.

of His prophesied origin. He will be found in a temporary dwelling like an alien who travels through the land, and He will be found in the manger and wrapped in swaddling cloths like a child of one of the shepherds themselves.[110]

The sign at the heart of the angel's message to the shepherds is the great secret of the Incarnation: that the promised Messiah, the Lamb of God, the Shepherd of Israel, the Son of David, the Savior who is Christ the Lord, is born not as the grandiose heir of a royal princedom but as one of you—an ordinary shepherd of Bethlehem, and you'll know this because He is just over yonder in the next village in a cave house just like yours, wrapped in swaddling cloths just like your babies, and lying in a manger—where you would place your newborn infants.

No wonder St. Luke includes the detail that everyone who heard about this was amazed. The long-awaited Messiah was born as a humble shepherd like His ancestor David. The Lord was present among them: the one the prophet Isaiah called "Emmanuel—God is with us."[111]

[110]Charles H Giblin, S.J., "Reflections on the Sign of the Manger," *Catholic Biblical Quarterly* 29 (1967): 87.
[111]See Isa. 7:14; Matt. 1:23.

Chapter 9

Mary Kept All These Things

When we hear the story of Jesus' birth read at Christmas, it is so familiar that we take certain details for granted, but when we meditate on the text in more depth certain details grab our attention. One of these is St. Luke's almost casual observation, "But Mary kept all these things, pondering them in her heart."[112]

The Blessed Virgin Mary welcomed the shepherds when they came to worship her newborn Child, and this alone must have been a reason for her to treasure the memories and ponder their meaning. The fact that she did carry these memories has been used as evidence that Mary herself is St. Luke's eyewitness for the events of Jesus' conception and birth. This is a venerable Catholic tradition that is illustrated by other beautiful legends. There is another tradition that St. Luke was not only a doctor, a writer, and

[112]Luke 2:19.

a traveling companion of St. Paul but also an artist and that he painted a portrait of the Virgin Mary. Four famous icons that are venerated today lay claim to being either the authentic portrait of Mary by St. Luke or a faithful copy of the original. Two of them are in Rome (at Santa Maria Maggiore and at the Church of St Alphonsus Liguori), one is in Russia (Our Lady of Vladimir), and one is in Poland (Our Lady of Czestochowa).

There is no external evidence and nothing in the Bible that supports the legend that St. Luke met the Virgin Mary and heard her story. The events Luke relates are so intimate, however, that it makes us wonder who else but Mary herself would have had such information. By the time Luke was writing, St. Joseph had passed away.

In a very conservative culture like first-century Judaism, it seems unlikely that anyone else would have known the true circumstances of Mary's virginity and Joseph's faithful, celibate relationship with her.

Modernist scholars argue that the whole story was borrowed from pagan myths of virgin births in order to boost the supernatural aspects of the Gospel and bolster Jesus' reputation as the Son of God. This seems unlikely because the early Christians were Jewish, and they felt an instinctive repugnance toward the surrounding pagan culture.

We should conclude that the story of the virginal conception and birth are rooted in real memories of real people concerning real events. Even with the latest possible dating of the Gospels (around AD 70–80), there was not enough time for the stories to have evolved sufficiently for a mythical virgin-birth story to have been added to the tale. By the time the Gospels were written down, there were enough people still living to have corrected the intentional addition of extraordinary, pagan, mythical elements. Instead, we should ask again, "Who would have known such intimate details?"

At the beginning of his Gospel St. Luke says, "Inasmuch as many have undertaken to compile a narrative of the things which have been accomplished among us, just as they were delivered to us by those who from the beginning were eyewitnesses and ministers of the word, it seemed good to me also, having followed all things closely for some time past, to write an orderly account for you."[113] From this, we can see, first, that before Luke was writing, there were others who had also written down what had happened. St. Luke used their eyewitness accounts and did his own investigations. To whom did he talk? What did those investigations consist of?

[113] Luke 1:1–3.

Mary and Joseph would have known the intimate details, and although we do not have explicit evidence, it is not impossible that St. Matthew knew St. Joseph and recorded his memories of the events, nor is it impossible that St. Luke met the Virgin Mary and recorded her memories.[114] Certainly this was the tradition of the early Church.

There are others, however, who would have known what happened. Mary's kinswoman Elizabeth and her husband, Zechariah, would have known. Mary went to spend three months with them immediately after the conception of Jesus, and although we cannot take it as absolute historical evidence, the *Protoevangelium of James* links Zechariah with Joseph and Mary's betrothal. Simply from Mary's visitation to Elizabeth, we can conclude a level of intimacy such that Elizabeth and Zechariah would have known the details. By the time the Gospels came to be written, they would have died, but their knowledge of Mary's unique pregnancy and the circumstances of Jesus' birth would have been shared with their son, John the Baptist, who may have passed on the information to his disciples; and many of John's disciples became followers of Jesus and then members of the early Christian community in Jerusalem.

[114]Bauckham, "Luke's Infancy Narrative as Oral History," 402.

The others who would have known the stories of the Annunciation and Joseph's dreams were the extended family members of Mary and Joseph.

We know from the Acts of the Apostles that James "the brother of Jesus" was the leader of the early Church in Jerusalem. Luke was a traveling companion of St. Paul, and Acts 21:18 tells us that they went to Jerusalem and met James. Richard Bauckham suggests, "In the succeeding period he would have had ample opportunity to speak with James and quite plausibly also with the other relatives of Jesus."[115] Bauckham goes on to present evidence for an early Church tradition that the family members of Jesus — active in the Christian community in Jerusalem — were involved in preaching the Gospel. There are linguistic links that the genealogy of Jesus that Luke records has links with the genealogies that the relatives of Jesus used in their preaching.[116]

We will never know for certain who informed St. Luke about the events leading to the births of John the Baptist and of Jesus, but there are enough hints, clues, and fragments of knowledge to take seriously the tradition that the Virgin Mary is the root source.

[115] Ibid., 407
[116] Ibid., 408.

If St. Luke did not meet her in person and paint her picture, then she was the ground-level source of information. We know she was present on Pentecost and therefore centrally involved with the first Christians in the Church in Jerusalem.

Mary may not have told the story directly to St. Luke, but she treasured the details in her heart and would have shared them with the apostles, who would have shared them with the first Christians in Jerusalem. These first Christians would have included members of Jesus' extended family and the disciples of John the Baptist, who would have passed on the stories he had heard from his parents, Elizabeth and Zechariah.

How this transmission of oral history takes place is a fascinating study. In our modern world, where the written word is so important, and where we have the technology to record events in written, audio and video format, we have lost the technique for accurately handing on oral traditions from one generation to another.

We imagine that oral tradition will be inaccurate, exaggerated, and elaborated. We distrust eyewitnesses because we know how events can be misrepresented and distorted due to "Chinese whispers" or the injection of some political, religious, or ideological agenda. In ancient societies, where illiteracy was the norm, however, maintaining accurate oral methods of handing on the stories and activities of the past was vitally important.

It is the study of how oral traditions are passed on that brings us to the secret of why the Bethlehem shepherds were so important to St. Luke—and if to St. Luke, then also to us today.

Chapter 10

The Shepherds as Witnesses

To understand the importance of the Bethlehem shepherds, we need to take time to understand how the Gospels were formed. For thousands of years, it was simply assumed that that the authors of Scripture were inspired by the Holy Spirit, as if God dictated the Scriptures to them word for word.

The Scriptures are indeed inspired by the Holy Spirit, but the Spirit speaks in and through human history, particular circumstances, the contemporary cultures, and the individual gifts, language, experiences, and knowledge of the authors. The Scriptures are therefore a picture of the Incarnation itself, and the Christmas story is the perfect illustration: God's Son comes into the world not as some alien being or superhero whose feet scarcely touch the ground but as an ordinary child of working-class parents, born in a simple cave house, wrapped in swaddling cloths, and laid in a manger—just as the shepherds' children would have been.

If you like, the angel message is this: "The Messiah has come, and he is a Bethlehem shepherd like you."

So the Scriptures are also born within and through the ordinary particular circumstances of first-century Palestine. It was only after the Enlightenment in Europe that scholars began to move away from the idea of supernaturally dictated Scriptures that were imposed on the world and began to understand how the Scriptures were inspired from within the culture, customs, and human personalities of the authors.

Unfortunately, this understanding was very often linked with an intentionally antisupernatural mentality. Rather than seeing the Holy Spirit's work welling up from within and through the personalities and circumstances of the authors, they taught that the Scriptures were *only* the product of the authors' imaginations and the cultural influences.

As a result, modern scholars suspected that all the supernatural aspects of the Bible stories were fanciful imaginative stories. They tried to weed out the supernatural from the ethical teachings and the historical fragments. Biblical critics such as Rudolf Bultmann called this process *demythologization* because it attempted to sift out the "mythological-supernatural" aspects of the Gospels.

As part of the attempt to understand how we got the Scriptures, the scholars proposed that the Gospels were only the product of the early Church and that they were documents of primarily theological truths and moral teaching rather than historical records of Jesus' life, ministry, death, and Resurrection.

These scholars were called "form critics" because they examined the forms and formation of the Gospel passages. In addition to the influences of the early Church, they traced possible influences on the development of the Scriptures from Jewish and secular sources—pagan religions, Greek philosophy, Roman poets, and so forth.

While form criticism was developing in the academic world of the early twentieth century, several other areas of academic interest were new and flourishing. Anthropology and archaeology, the study of ancient cultures, was growing. This was accompanied by the study of religion, mythology, and folklore.

Bultmann found "laws of tradition," or the way traditions were passed on within folktales, popular proverbs and anecdotes, narrative poetry, and folk songs. The traditions developed within the community over a long period,and as they developed, Bultmann reasoned, they accumulated levels of legend and myth. Furthermore, this method of development was one of gradual evolution within the community. "For the form critics it was axiomatic that folk literature was anonymous and to be attributed to the community, not to individuals, certainly not named individuals."[117] This is why, if you do research on the Gospels, you will find that modernist biblical scholars usually say that Matthew's Gospel was written not by Matthew but by some anonymous member of the community a long time after the events took place.

Because they concluded that the Gospels originated from within the early Christian community, they assumed that the only purpose for the Gospels was theological and moral teaching. Consequently, the critics concluded that the early Christian Church had no real interest in the historical accuracy of the Gospels and didn't care whether there were eyewitnesses.[118]

The conclusion most scholars and students of the New Testament came away with is that there was a long period of oral tradition after the Gospel events, and during that period, the stories developed, were elaborated and exaggerated, and absorbed supernatural elements so that by the time they came to be written down, there was very little historical content left; there was, at best, a fragment of the truth,

[117] Richard Bauckham, *Jesus and the Eyewitnesses: The Gospels as Eyewitness Testimony* (Grand Rapids: Eerdmans, 2006), 245.
[118] Ibid. p. 246

distorted and broken by the process of development. Now, a hundred years later, Richard Bauckham asserts, "Virtually every element in this construction has been questioned and rejected by some or even most scholars."[119]

As with most radical ideas, there was a swing in the other direction. In the 1960s, the Swedish scholar Birger Gerhardsson researched Jewish methods of teaching and transmitting traditions. He discovered that "disciples of rabbis were expected to memorize their master's teaching, and importance was attached to preserving the exact words."[120] Yet an in-depth study shows that the Gospels are not the result simply of word-for-word memorization. The sayings of Jesus were probably the result of memorization, but the stories of His actions and the narrative of His passion are more open-ended.

By the 1990s, a middle way between the free-flowing, informal development of Bultmann and the rigid memorization theory of Gerhardsson had developed. Kenneth Bailey, whom we have already met with his ideas about typical Palestinian homes, lived and worked in the Holy Land for more than thirty years. He observed oral tradition at work

[119]Ibid.
[120]Ibid.

among the local inhabitants and discerned three ways the locals passed on their stories and traditions:

1. *Informal uncontrolled* oral tradition: This is simply informal anecdotes, jokes, or even gossip.
2. *Formal controlled* oral tradition: This involves memorizing and reciting the traditional story or passage of tradition, and the elders and teachers (along with the hearers) correct the person reciting the tradition if he makes a mistake.
3. *Informal controlled* oral tradition: In this transmission of tradition, the community may be gathered around the fire for the telling of a traditional story. The storyteller may elaborate and add drama or characterization, but if he departs from the essential facts, the elders and teachers (and the whole community) correct him.

Explaining Bailey's discoveries, Richard Bauckham summarizes, "In this model it is the community that exercises control to ensure that their traditions are preserved faithfully."[121]

Noted New Testament scholar N. T. Wright explains further: "Bailey divides the traditions into five categories: proverbs, poetry, narrative riddles, parables and stories of

[121] Ibid., 255.

important historical figures. Poems and proverbs allow no flexibility. Some flexibility is allowed within parables and recollections of historical figures but the central threads of the story cannot be changed."[122]

This outline of how the Gospel stories were passed on is important for understanding the role of the Bethlehem shepherds. If we remember that the seminomadic shepherds of Bethlehem are essentially a Bedouin culture, it is not surprising to discover that the Bedouin transmit their stories and traditions in the same way that Kenneth Bailey describes.

Another Bailey—Clinton Bailey—also spent decades living and working in the Holy Land. His special area of research and expertise is Bedouin culture. He records the different ways in which the Bedouin transmit their oral traditions. They have proverbs and narrative poetry, which are very formal and must be memorized, and they rely on genealogies, which must also be memorized.

They also use prose storytelling and histories of their important tribal characters; this allows for some flexibility, leaving room for personal flourishes, humor, and characterization.

[122]N. T. Wright, *Jesus and the Victory of God* (Minneapolis: Fortress Press, 1996), 134–135.

the additions or elaboration cannot alter the basic content of the story, however, and it is the elders and the community members who work together to monitor the traditions to maintain accuracy of the essential facts.

When we put these factors together, we can see why the shepherds were important: in addition to whatever St. Luke may have gleaned from the members of the early Church in Jerusalem—who knew Jesus' extended family members—the shepherds of Bethlehem were the primary sources for Luke's story. They were eyewitnesses. Luke says that the shepherds passed on what they had seen: "When they saw it they made known the saying which had been told them concerning this child; and all who heard it wondered at what the shepherds told them."[123]

All the details are there. As explained in Clinton Bailey's study of Bedouin culture, the shepherds memorized and retold the genealogy of the Baby as they learned it from their neighbors: Joseph and his relatives. The message and song of the angels are told in poetic form and therefore also relied on word-for-word memorization, but the story itself adds characterization and dialogue: "Let us go over

[123] Luke 2:17-18.

to Bethlehem and see this thing that has happened, which the Lord has made known to us."[124] The repetition of the important phrase, "wrapped in swaddling cloths and lying in a manger"[125] indicates a crucial element of the story that had to be memorized because it was a "sign." It was also a sign that this part of the story could not be forgotten.

Does this mean that St. Luke met the shepherds and interviewed them? As with his possible meeting with the Virgin Mary, it is improbable but not impossible. It is more likely that the shepherds continued to share the good news and that their methods of oral tradition kept the story alive so that fifty or sixty years after the event, St. Luke spoke to members of the early Church in Bethlehem—some of whom were descendants of the shepherds.

We know that centuries later, when the empress Helena discovered the birthplace of Christ, it was identified because the local people remembered the exact site. There is another intriguing hint that helps us recognize the secret of the shepherds. The town where we find the Shepherds' Fields is next to Bethlehem. It is not, however, called Bethlehem; it is called Beit Sahour.

[124]Luke 2:15.
[125]See Luke 2:7, 12.

In Hebrew *Bethlehem* means "House of Bread," but in Arabic and Aramaic, it means "House of Flesh." *Beit Sahour*—the shepherd's town next to Bethlehem—means "House of Those Who Stay Awake" or "House of the Nightwatch." Beit Sahour was named in tribute to the shepherds who were "keeping watch over their flock by night." The secret of the Bethlehem shepherds is not only that they were the first eyewitnesses of the Gospel but that they were also the ones who kept alive their story and shared it with others who shared it with St. Luke so that it was recorded for posterity.

Bibliography

Bailey, Clinton. *Bedouin Culture in the Bible*. New Haven: Yale University Press, 2018.

Bailey, Kenneth E. *Jesus through Middle Eastern Eyes: Cultural Studies in the Gospels*. Downers Grove, IL: IVP Academic, 2008.

Bailey, M. "The Crib and Exegesis of Luke 2:1–20," *Irish Ecclesiastical Review* 100, (1963): 358–376.

——. "The Shepherds and the Sign of a Child in the Manger." *Irish Theological Quarterly* 31 (1964): 1–23.

Barclay, John, and John Sweet, eds. *Early Christian Thought in Its Jewish Context*. Cambridge: Cambridge University Press, 1996.

Barker, Margaret. *Christmas: The Original Story*. London: Society for Promoting Christian Knowledge, 2018.

——. *Temple Theology, An Introduction*. London: Society for Promoting Christian Knowledge, 2004.

——. "The Temple Roots of the Christian Liturgy." *Journal for the Study of the New Testament* (2003).

Bar-On, Shimon. "The Development of the Tamid Offering and Its Place in the Priestly Calendar of Sacrifice." *Proceedings of the Twelfth World Congress of Jewish Studies* (1997).

Barrois, Georges A. *Jesus Christ and the Temple.* Crestwood, NY: St. Vladimir Seminary Press, 1980.

Bauckham, Richard. *Jesus and the Eyewitnesses: The Gospels as Eyewitness Testimony.* Grand Rapids: Eerdmans, 2006.

——. "Luke's Infancy Narrative as Oral History In *The Gospels: History and Christology: The Search of Joseph Ratzinger–Benedict XVI*, edited by Bernardo Estrada, Ermenegildo Manicardi, and Armand Puig i Tàrrech. Citta del Vaticano: Libreria Editrice Vaticana, 2013.

Betz, Otto. "The Essenes." In *Judaism.* Vol. 3, *The Early Roman Period.* Edited by William Horbury, W. D. Davies, and John Sturdy. Cambridge: Cambridge University Press, 1999.

Borg, Marcus J., and John Dominic Crossian. *The First Christmas: What the Gospels Really Teach about Jesus's Birth.* San Francisco: HarperOne, 2007.

Bovon, François. *Luke 1: A Commentary on the Gospel of Luke 1:1-9:50.* Translated by Christine M. Thomas. Edited by Helmut Koester. Minneapolis: Fortress Press, 2002.

Broder, Jonathan. "Shepherds' Caves Still Dot the Holy Land." *Chicago* Tribune, December 25, 1987. https://www.chicagotribune.com/news/ct-xpm-1987-12-25-8704050765-story.html.

Brown, Raymond E. *The Birth of the Messiah: A Commentary on the Infancy Narratives of Matthew and Luke.* New York: Doubleday, 1993.

Buttrick, George Arthur, ed. *The Interpreter's Bible*. Vol. 8, *Luke and John*. New York: Abingdon Press, 1952.

Carlson, Stephen C. "The Accommodation of Joseph and Mary in Bethlehem." *New Testament Studies* 56, no. 3 (May 2010): 326–342.

Coloe, Mary L. " 'Behold the Lamb of God': John 1:29 and the Tamid Service. In *Rediscovering John: Essays on the Fourth Gospel in Honor of Frédéric Manns*, edited by L. Daniel Chrupcala, 337–350. Milan: Edizioni Terra Santa, 2013.

Creed, J. M. *The Gospel according to St Luke*. London: Macmillan, 1942.

Davis, John J. *The Perfect Shepherd: Studies in the Twenty-Third Psalm*. Grand Rapids: Baker Book House, 1979.

Derrett, J. D. M. "The Manger at Bethlehem: Light on St. Luke's Technique from Contemporary Jewish Religious Law." *Studies in the New Testament* 2 (1978): 39–47.

——. "The Manger: Ritual Law and Soteriology." *Theology* 74 (1971): 566–571.

Easton, Burton Scott. *The Gospel according to St. Luke: A Critical and Exegetical Commentary*. New York: Scribner, 1926.

Edersheim, Alfred. *The Life and Times of Jesus the Messiah*. New York: Longmans Green, 1901.

——. *The Temple, Its Ministry and Services as They Were at the Time of Jesus Christ*. London: Religious Tract Society, 1903.

Epstein, H. "Awassi Sheep." Food and Agricultural Organization of the United Nations. https://www.fao.org/3/p8550e/P8550E01.htm.

Estrada, Bernardo, Ermenegildo Manicardi, and Armand Puig i Tàrrech. *The Gospels: History and Christology: The Search of Joseph Ratzinger–Benedict XVI.* Citta del Vaticano: Libreria Editrice Vaticana, 2013.

Eusebius. *History of the Church.* In *A Select Library of Nicene and Post-Nicene Fathers.* Grand Rapids: T&T Clark, 1991.

Fitzmyer, Joseph A., S.J. *The Gospel according to St. Luke.* New York: Doubleday, 1979.

France, R. T. "The Birth of Jesus." In *Handbook for the Study of the Historical Jesus*, vol. 3, edited by Tom Holmén and Stanley E. Porter. Boston: Brill, 2011.

Frenken, Ralph. "Psychology and History of Swaddling, Part Two: The Abolishment of Swaddling from the 16th Century until Today." *Journal of Psychohistory* 39, no. 3 (Winter 2012): 219–245.

Geldenhuys, Norval. *The Gospel of Luke.* The New International Commentary on the New Testament. Grand Rapids: Eerdmans, 1988.

Giblin, C. H. "Reflections on the Sign of the Manger." *Catholic Biblical Quarterly* 29 (1967): 87–101.

Ginzberg, Louis. "Tamid: The Oldest Treatise of the Mishnah." *Journal of Jewish Lore and Philosophy* (1919).

Goodman, Martin. "The Temple in First Century CE Judaism." In *Temple and Worship in Biblical Israel*, edited by John Day, 459-468. London: T&T Clark, 2005.

Hamm, Denis. "The Tamid Service in Luke-Acts: The Cultic Background behind Luke's Theology of Worship" *Catholic Biblical Quarterly* 65, no. 2 (April 2003): 215–231.

Horsley, Richard. *Galilee-History, Politics, People*. Valley Forge, PA: Trinity Press, 1995.

Huebner, Sabine. *Papyri and the Social World of the New Testament*. Cambridge: Cambridge University Press, 2019.

Hunt, Michal E. *Jesus and the Mystery of the Tamid Sacrifice*. Self-published, 2020.

Jeremias, Joachim. *Jerusalem in the Time of Jesus*. London: SCM Press, 1967.

Joseph, Simon. *Jesus, The Essenes and Christian Origins: New Light on Ancient Texts and Communities*. Waco, TX: Baylor University Press, 2018.

Josephus, Flavius. *The New Complete Works of Josephus*. Translated by William Whiston. Grand Rapids: Kregel, 1999.

Kealey, Sean. *The Gospel of Luke*. Montclair, NJ: Dimension Books, 1979.

Kittel, Gerhard. *The Theological Dictionary of the New Testament*. Vols. 6, 7. Translated by G. Bromley. Grand Rapids: Eerdmans, 1968.

Legrand, L. "The Way of the Magi and the Way of the Shepherds." *Indian Theological Studies* 30, no. 4 (1993): 313–318.

Levine, Amy-Jill, and Ben Witherington III. *The Gospel of Luke*. New Cambridge Bible Commentary. Cambridge: Cambridge University Press, 2018.

Liefeld, Walter. *The Expositor's Bible Commentary*. Grand Rapids: Zondervan, 1984.

Marshall, I. Howard. *The Gospel of Luke: A Commentary on the Greek Text*. Exeter, England: Paternoster Press, 1978.

———. *Luke: Historian and Theologian*. Downers Grove: InterVarsity Press, 1970.

Mason, Steve. "Where Was Jesus Born? O Little Town of ... Nazareth?" *Bible Review* 16 no. 1 (February 2000): 31–39.

Meyers, Eric. *Galilee through the Centuries*. Winona Lake, IN: Eisenbrauns, 1999.

The Mishnah: A New Translation. Translated by Jacob Neusner. London: Yale University Press, 1988.

Murphy-O'Connor, Jerome. *The Holy Land: An Oxford Archeological Guide from Earliest Times to 1700*. Oxford: Oxford University Press, 1998.

———. "Where Was Jesus Born? Bethlehem ... of Course." *Bible Review* 16, no. 1 (February 2000): 40–45, 50.

Nestle, Eberhard. "The Bethlehem Shepherds." *Expository Times* 17, (1906).

Nolland, John. *World Biblical Commentary*. Dallas: Word Books, 1989.

Perowne, Stuart. *The Pilgrim's Companion in Jerusalem and Bethlehem*. London: Hodder and Stoughton, 1964.

Puig i Tàrrech, Armand. "The Birth of Jesus and History: The Interweaving of the Infancy Narratives in Matthew and Luke."

In *The Gospels: History and Christology: The Search of Joseph Ratzinger–Benedict XVI*, edited by Bernardo Estrada, Ermenegildo Manicardi, and Armand Puig i Tàrrech. Citta del Vaticano: Libreria Editrice Vaticana, 2013.

Porter, Stanley. "The Witness of Extra-Gospel Literary Sources to the Infancy Narratives of the Synoptic Gospels." In *The Gospels: History and Christology: The Search of Joseph Ratzinger–Benedict XVI*, edited by Bernardo Estrada, Ermenegildo Manicardi, and Armand Puig i Tàrrech. Citta del Vaticano: Libreria Editrice Vaticana, 2013.

Plummer, Rev. Alfred. *A Critical and Exegetical Commentary on the Gospel according to St. Luke*. 4th ed. Edinburgh: T&T Clark, 1910.

Protoevangelium of James. Translated by Alexander Walker. In *Ante-Nicene Fathers*, vol. 8. Edited by Alexander Roberts, James Donaldson, and A. Cleveland Coxe. Buffalo: Christian Literature Publishing, 1886. Revised and edited for New Advent by Kevin Knight. https://www.newadvent.org/fathers/0847.htm.

Ratzinger, Joseph/Pope Benedict XVI. *Jesus of Nazareth: The Infancy Narratives*. New York: Image Books, 2018.

Reisner, Rainer. "Bethlehem: The Birth Stories and Archaeology in Matthew and Luke." In *The Gospels: History and Christology: The Search of Joseph Ratzinger–Benedict XVI*, edited by Bernardo Estrada, Ermenegildo Manicardi, and Armand Puig i Tàrrech. Citta del Vaticano: Libreria Editrice Vaticana, 2013.

Safrai, S., and M. Stern in cooperation with D. Flusser and W. C. van Unnik. *The Jewish People in the First Century: Historical Geography, Political History, Social, Cultural, and Religious Life and Institutions.* Assen: Van Gorcum, 1974.

Schmidt, Ekhart David. "Luke's Census under Quirinius: A Case for Historians, Tax Lawyers and Theologians." In *The Gospels: History and Christology: The Search of Joseph Ratzinger–Benedict XVI*, edited by Bernardo Estrada, Ermenegildo Manicardi, and Armand Puig i Tàrrech. Citta del Vaticano: Libreria Editrice Vaticana, 2013.

The Tosefta: Translated from the Hebrew with a New Introduction. Translated by Jacob Neusner. Peabody, MA: Hendrickson, 2002.

Tyson, Joseph B. *Images of Judaism in Luke-Acts.* Columbia: University of South Carolina Press, 1991.

Winter, Paul. "The Cultural Background of the Narrative in Luke I and II." *Jewish Quarterly Review* 45–46 (1955).

Wallace, J. Warner. "Is Mark's Gospel an Early Memoir of the Apostle Peter?" Christianity.com, January 17, 2014. https://www.christianity.com/blogs/j-warner-wallace/is-marks-gospel-an-early-memoir-of-the-apostle-peter.html.

Wright, N. T. *Jesus and the Victory of God.* Minneapolis: Fortress Press, 1996.

About the Author

Fr. Dwight Longenecker was brought up in an Evangelical home in Pennsylvania and studied English and speech at Bob Jones University before being trained for ministry in the Church of England at Oxford. He served for fifteen years as an Anglican priest before he and his family were received into the Catholic Church.

In 2006, Fr. Longenecker returned to the United States to be ordained a Catholic priest under the pastoral provision for married former Protestant ministers. He now serves as the pastor of Our Lady of the Rosary parish in Greenville, South Carolina. He is married to Alison, and they have four grown children.

Fr. Longenecker is the author of more than twenty books on Catholic Faith and culture. His blog, *Standing on My Head*, is one of the most widely read Catholic blogs. Fr.

Longenecker also contributes to a wide range of magazines, journals, websites, and podcasts. You can follow his writings, listen to his podcasts, join his online courses, browse his books, and be in touch at DwightLongenecker.com.

Sophia Institute

Sophia Institute is a nonprofit institution that seeks to nurture the spiritual, moral, and cultural life of souls and to spread the gospel of Christ in conformity with the authentic teachings of the Roman Catholic Church.

Sophia Institute Press fulfills this mission by offering translations, reprints, and new publications that afford readers a rich source of the enduring wisdom of mankind.

Sophia Institute also operates the popular online resource CatholicExchange.com. *Catholic Exchange* provides world news from a Catholic perspective as well as daily devotionals and articles that will help readers to grow in holiness and live a life consistent with the teachings of the Church.

In 2013, Sophia Institute launched Sophia Institute for Teachers to renew and rebuild Catholic culture through service to Catholic education. With the goal of nurturing the spiritual, moral, and cultural life of souls, and an abiding respect for the role and work of teachers, we strive to provide materials and programs that are at once enlightening to the mind and ennobling to the heart; faithful and complete, as well as useful and practical.

Sophia Institute gratefully recognizes the Solidarity Association for preserving and encouraging the growth of our apostolate over the course of many years. Without their generous and timely support, this book would not be in your hands.

www.SophiaInstitute.com
www.CatholicExchange.com
www.SophiaInstituteforTeachers.org

Sophia Institute Press® is a registered trademark of Sophia Institute. Sophia Institute is a tax-exempt institution as defined by the Internal Revenue Code, Section 501(c)(3). Tax ID 22-2548708.